Ubuntu Pocket Guide and Reference

Keir Thomas

MacFreda
Publishing

Ubuntu Pocket Guide and Reference (Print Edition)
Version: CS1.0
www.ubuntupocketguide.com

Copyright © 2009 by Keir Thomas
All rights reserved.

ISBN (EAN-13): 9781440478291

Contents

About the author

Keir Thomas is the one of the world's most prolific authors writing about Ubuntu Linux.

Ubuntu Pocket Guide and Reference is his third Ubuntu book, and his award-winning comprehensive guide to Ubuntu—*Beginning Ubuntu Linux* (ISBN 978-1590599914)—recently reached a third edition.

Thomas is also the author of *Ubuntu Kung Fu* (ISBN 978-1934356227), a unique book containing over 300 tips, tricks, hints, and hacks for Ubuntu. It regularly tops the Amazon.com best-seller list in the Linux category.

He has written books on the subjects of SUSE and Fedora Linux, and edited books on subjects ranging from enterprise e-commerce to Ruby programming. In a previous life he edited several top-selling computer magazines, including *PC Utilities* and *Linux User & Developer*, and has written for many more.

He lives in the United Kingdom and his pastimes include hiking, cycling, and gardening.

He wishes to thank the technical reviewers of this book: John Southern, Matthew Helmke, and Ryan Troy.

A brief introduction

The purpose of this chapter is to introduce you to the Ubuntu operating system, and the philosophy that underpins it.

The fact you're reading this book might mean you already know about Ubuntu, but one or two readers might have bought the Print Edition of this book (or downloaded the PDF) on a whim to see what the fuss is all about. These people might lack specifics, and remain unconvinced of the benefits of Ubuntu. So, I'm going to burn through some precious pages of this slim volume to evangelize and explain just a little.

What is Ubuntu?

Ubuntu is a version of the Linux operating system. An operating system is the software that "runs your computer". Microsoft Windows is the world's most popular operating system, at least for desktop computers, but Linux is a completely separate endeavor.

GNU

The ball started rolling back in the 1980s, when a hugely talented computer scientist called Richard Stallman decided to create a clone of a venerable operating system called Unix. At the time, Unix ran many of the world's industrial and academic computer systems.

Stallman did this because Unix was becoming increasingly *proprietary*—it was no longer permitted to share its source code (the listings created by programmers), as had happened since the inception of Unix in 1969.

This was anathema to Stallman, who believed sharing software was natural and healthy. He decided his version of Unix would always be freely available, and invented the legal and ethical concept of *Free Software* to ensure this happened. Put simply, Free Software says users should always have the freedom to share software, without restrictions. On a technical level, Free Software guarantees the right to view and also modify source code, or even use it as a basis to make a new program. However, any additions or changes must be released as Free Software too, so others can continue to benefit.

> **NOTE** The Free Software ideal is enshrined in a software license applied to all Free Software projects. It's called the *GNU Public License*, or GPL. This is like Microsoft's End User License Agreement that comes with Windows (and you see whenever you install Windows from scratch), except whereas the Microsoft EULA prohibits sharing Windows under any circumstances, the GPL says exactly the opposite—that you can *always* share the software!

Stallman called his version of Unix "GNU" (pronounced *G-noo*). This is a recursive acronym, standing for *GNU's Not Unix*. In other words, the acronym refers to itself—a joke of a type favored by programmers.

The Linux kernel

GNU grew into a major project with many contributors. However, good as it was, it lacked a *kernel*. A kernel is the program at the heart of any operating system that takes care of fundamental stuff, like letting hardware communicate with software.

Almost by accident, a chap called Linus Torvalds provided a solution. In 1991 he started a personal project to create a kernel. Due to a naming error when his kernel was uploaded to the Internet, it got named after him and became known as *Linux*—a hybrid of "Linus" and "Unix".

Crucially, Torvalds chose to release his kernel as Free Software, and invited any interested party to give him a hand. They did. Thousands of people around the world got involved. As the years went by, the project became more and more important, and grander in its design and outlook. Today, the Linux kernel receives sponsorship from many major corporations, including IBM.

> **NOTE** Torvalds continues to oversee and contribute to the Linux kernel project to this day. He humorously describes his role as a "benign dictator".

Because the kernel is such an important aspect of an operating system, people began to refer to the combination of GNU and Linux simply as *Linux*. This upset Stallman, who asked that the name GNU/Linux be used instead. But it was too late. The name stuck.

NOTE Whether to refer to the operating system as GNU/Linux or simply Linux is a debate that continues to this day.

Software from other sources is typically included in the Linux operating system too, alongside GNU and the Linux kernel. Virtually all the software in Linux is Free Software, even though much of it has no direct ties with GNU or Richard Stallman. Arguably, Stallman's greatest gift to the world was not the GNU software, but the concept of Free Software. Much of Stallman's activity nowadays involves evangelizing around the world about Free Software.

NOTE Often the term *open source* is used instead of Free Software. It has a similar meaning—see www.opensource.org.

Linux distros

There isn't just one version of Linux. There are hundreds. Versions are known as *distributions* of Linux, or *distros* for short. Examples of other distros include Red Hat (www.redhat.com) and SUSE (www.suse.com), but there are many others, and new ones appear all the time.

This variety is possible because of the freedom allowed by Free Software—anybody can take the source code and make their own version.

Some distros are commercially sponsored, while others arose from the massive community of Linux users around the world. Ubuntu is a little of both: it is sponsored by Canonical, a company founded by the entrepreneur Mark Shuttleworth in 2004, but it also benefits from massive community support, and is based on Debian (www.debian.org), a community-generated distro.

What makes Ubuntu special

Three things make Ubuntu stand out from the crowd:

1. Its focus on desktop users;

2. The Ubuntu philosophy and community;

3. Ease of use.

Let's take a closer look at each.

Focus on desktop users

Although it comes in versions for all kinds of computers, at its core Ubuntu is a distribution of Linux aimed primarily at desktop users.

Most Linux distros are equally at home on desktop or server computers (the powerful computers that run the Internet), but lack polish when it comes to the desktop experience. Indeed, in many cases the needs of desktop users are something of an afterthought.

In contrast, the desktop experience is something to which the Ubuntu developers pay very close attention.

When Ubuntu was created back in 2004, Mark Shuttleworth recorded the very first bug in the online database. However, it wasn't about software. Instead, it was a revolutionary call to arms. It read as follows: "Microsoft has a majority market share in the new desktop PC marketplace. This is a bug, which Ubuntu is designed to fix".

Philosophy and community

As you might have realized, Linux is as much a philosophy as it is an operating system. Ubuntu is no different.

African values

Ubuntu gets its title from the African concept of the same name that translates roughly as "humanity to others". The term gained popularity in post-apartheid South Africa, where it stressed the importance of individuals recognizing their role within communities, and being generous of spirit because of this.

When Mark Shuttleworth founded the Ubuntu Linux project in 2004, he drew-up a philosophical statement, based on this concept, and on the principles of Free Software.

In a nutshell, the Ubuntu project is driven by the idea that software should be inclusive. It should be possible for anybody, anywhere to use, share, or modify Ubuntu. This means the software should be available in a particular user's language too. If they have a disability, the software should be accessible to them.

Ubuntu is free of charge, like nearly all versions of Linux. Updates are also free-of-charge for a set period after release (usually 18 months, but see the table on page 7 for more details).

NOTE You can read more about the Ubuntu philosophy at www.ubuntu.com/community/ubuntustory/philosophy, and read more about the Free Software Foundation's principles at www.gnu.org/philosophy/free-sw.html.

What Ubuntu represents is *freedom*—freedom to use and share the software, to do what you want with it, and to learn.

The community

The Ubuntu community arose directly out of the Ubuntu philosophy. Put simply, people respect the principled stand Ubuntu takes. They also like the fact that Ubuntu focuses on the desktop experience.

There have been many versions of Linux that, like Ubuntu, were aimed specifically at desktop users. Virtually all failed. This was because they compromised on some component of Free Software principles. Maybe their version of Linux included a proprietary installation program that couldn't be freely shared or modified. Sometimes they attempted to limit redistribution of their version of Linux.

Ubuntu doesn't do any of this. Its reward is a truly massive community of users around the world—arguably the biggest user-base of any version of Linux. It's certainly one of the friendliest Linux communities.

Shuttleworth takes a back seat and, apart from occasionally issuing edicts, the community runs the show. Decisions about new features are made democratically, and many of its users help develop Ubuntu (provided they have the skills, of course).

For a humble end-user of Ubuntu, the benefit of the Ubuntu community is found in the magnificent technical support offered at www.ubuntuforums.org, the community forums site where Ubuntu users hang-out and help each other.

NOTE It isn't 100% accurate that Ubuntu doesn't include proprietary software. A small amount of proprietary hardware firmware is provided to support wireless and graphics devices presently not fully supported by Free Software. This is seen a stopgap measure, however, until more acceptable alternatives become available.

Ease of use

Alongside strong principles and financial sponsorship, Shuttleworth brought something else to the Linux party: He wanted to make a "Linux for human beings". Indeed, this is Ubuntu's tag line.

How it used to be

To understand why this is important, let me recount an experience I had with Linux in 2002, before Ubuntu hit the scene. I wanted the wireless card in my notebook to connect to my network, but I couldn't get it working under Linux. So, I asked for help on a popular forum. I received something similar to the following in reply:

> *"Getting the card to work is simple! Just grab the source code for the module and compile it against the kernel.* insmod *it and then use* iwconfig *to configure a WEP password—"*

Are you still reading? As you can tell, that's a complex answer. It involves working at the command-line, and requires knowledge of how Linux works on a very technical level. I knew what the poster was talking about, although inwardly I sighed at the amount of work involved. However, a newcomer would be baffled.

That's how it was back then. Linux was "for techies only". It was considered an industrial-strength operating system, and brought with it a steep learning curve that drove many away.

How it is now

Ubuntu changed everything. It focuses on the desktop user experience and, to this end, features graphical configuration software. It includes a wide variety of hardware drivers so that nearly all standard hardware "just works". Ubuntu comes with an installer program that doesn't feature mind-boggling terminology, and updating the system takes just a few clicks of the mouse.

> **NOTE** To be fair, it can be argued Ubuntu was part of a broader revolution in desktop Linux, and several other versions of Linux were heading in the same direction. Ubuntu was the first to get there, and continues to lead the charge with each new release.

While the command-line is still around, there's no longer an obligatory requirement to use it. It's often quicker and more efficient to use it, as you'll find out later in this book, but you don't have to. Ubuntu makes Linux truly accessible to all.

Don't think Ubuntu is somehow "less Linux" than other versions. Scratch under the surface and you'll find Ubuntu is based on Debian, a widely-respected community-generated version of Linux that many consider definitive. See www.debian.org.

What Ubuntu offers

Ubuntu is a thoroughly modern operating system that provides everything you might find in Windows or Macintosh OS X, but without the drawbacks. It keeps things simple, yet offers sophisticated features.

Want to browse the web? Firefox will do the job. This is the same Firefox you might have been using under Windows and, yes, the same add-ons will work. Want to instant-message friends using AIM, MSN, or ICQ? Pidgin provides the solution. Need to do some word-processing, or spreadsheeting, or presenting? OpenOffice.org will do the trick. GIMP will handle image-editing, while RhythmBox will take care of music playback (stand-alone video playback is handled by Totem).

All of these programs are installed by default. They're not extras and they're all free of charge.

Hardware support is excellent, with virtually every item of day-to-day hardware supported, including graphics/sound cards, printers, wireless, USB memory sticks, cameras, iPods, and so-on. There's no need to fumble around with driver CDs—practically everything will be up and running straight after installation, although as with any operating system you may have to configure the system to your own tastes and needs.

> **TIP** Ubuntu works well on older hardware. The minimum realistic requirements for Ubuntu 8.04 are a 700MHz processor, 384MB of memory, and 8GB of disk space. You might consider installing Ubuntu on an older PC to evaluate it, before installing it on your day-to-day computer.

How to read this book

Ubuntu Pocket Guide and Reference is concise. Its goal is to explain the essentials of day-to-day Ubuntu administration in a fuss-free manner. Due to the limited size of the pocket book format, at times it can be a whistle-stop tour of Ubuntu features. However, topics are always fully explained, and often I linger over details to provide a lasting reference.

There are certainly more comprehensive Ubuntu books around. I recommend *Beginning Ubuntu Linux, Third Edition*, written by Jaime Sicam and myself. It's published by Apress (June 2008; ISBN 978-1590599914) and provides a complete guide to Ubuntu.

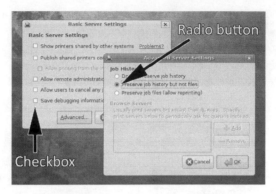

Figure i-1. Checkboxes and radio buttons.

Typing commands

Sometimes I might ask you type something at the command-line. Usually this will appear on a line of its own, like this:

- mv /home/keir/Desktop/report.doc /home/keir

Some commands are long and won't fit on a single line of the page. If this is the case, I use the following symbol at the end of the line: ⏎

Menu options

In some sections, I ask that you select a certain menu option. You might see something like the following: click System ⇨ Preferences ⇨ Appearance. What I mean is that you should click the System menu at the top of the screen, and then the Preferences submenu, and click the entry on that menu headed Appearance. It will be obvious what you have to do.

What to click

A quick word about *radio buttons* and *checkboxes*, both of which I reference throughout the book. Both are elements of dialog boxes, and activate certain functions. Radio buttons are usually round, while checkboxes are usually square. See Figure i-1 for an annotated example.

Ubuntu versions

This book was written using Ubuntu 8.10 as a base, and was further tested using the 8.04 long-term support release. Screenshots were taken using Ubuntu 8.10 and as such might differ slightly from what you see if using 8.04.

CHAPTER ONE

Installing Ubuntu

This chapter explains the methods used to install Ubuntu on a computer. Additionally, you'll learn how to:

- Choose a version (and release) of Ubuntu that's right for you;
- Undertake preparatory work to ensure that installation runs smoothly;
- Create your own Ubuntu installation CD-ROM;
- Install Ubuntu on problematic computers;
- Install Ubuntu on Intel-based Apple Macintosh computers.

Types of installation

Installing Ubuntu is much easier than you might think and there are essentially three ways of doing so, as follows:

#1: Dual-booting

If you intend to switch to Ubuntu full-time, installing Ubuntu by repartitioning your computer's hard disk is best. This involves shrinking the existing Windows partition and creating new partitions alongside for Ubuntu. Following this, Ubuntu is installed and a menu added so you can choose between Ubuntu and Windows at boot-time. Having Ubuntu and Windows side-by-side on a PC is called *dual-booting*.

This sounds complex, but it's automated via the Ubuntu installation software. However, there's a slight risk involved when repartitioning, so it's very wise to backup essential data first.

NOTE Instead of repartitioning, some users choose to wipe Windows from the hard disk and install Ubuntu in its place. This can also be done using the above installation method.

#2: Installing within Windows

Wubi is Windows software that installs Ubuntu within a series of virtual hard disk files contained in the Windows filesystem. It then configures a boot-time menu so you can choose between booting into Ubuntu or Windows. If you choose to boot into Ubuntu, a clever trick makes the virtual hard disk files appear to be real disks. As a result, the user will be entirely unaware they're not using a traditional partition-based installation, as described previously.

Using Wubi to install Ubuntu is just like installing some Windows software, and is equally risk-free. There's even an uninstall option added to Add/Remove Programs. The only drawback is a slight reduction in performance compared to a traditional installation, and you'll also find the Ubuntu suspend-to-disk (hibernate) power-saving mode doesn't work.

TIP You can still use the "sleep" power saving mode that suspends power to most of the computer's components except RAM.

#3: Virtual computer

By downloading a virtual computer application, such as the free-of-charge VMware Player (www.vmware.com/products/player), you can install Ubuntu so it runs within a program window on the Windows desktop.

A virtual computer is effectively a complete computer recreated in software. It offers an excellent way to trial Ubuntu, although the limitations of the virtual computer software mean you won't experience Ubuntu to its full advantage (desktop visual effects won't work, for example). Additionally, you'll need a powerful PC with over 1GB of memory for optimal results.

Preparing your PC for Ubuntu

Before installing Ubuntu, some preparatory work within Windows is advisable.

Ensuring enough disk space is free

Regardless of what installation method you choose, you'll need at least 5GB of free disk space for Ubuntu. For an installation you intend to use full-time, you'll probably need much more.

If your computer's hard disk is low on free disk space, you'll need to either uninstall some software using Add/Remove Programs in the Control Panel, or delete data. Multimedia files take-up most space.

Alternatively, if using a desktop PC, you can add an additional hard disk to your computer, onto which you can install Ubuntu. Unlike some versions of Windows, Ubuntu can be installed on disks that aren't the primary hard disk in the system.

> **TIP** Ubuntu 8.10 lets you install Ubuntu onto a USB memory stick, but performance is very poor and far from ideal for day-to-day use.

Defragmenting the hard disk

Once you're sure there's enough free space, you should defragment the hard disk. This is necessary because, if you use Wubi, you'll create some multi-gigabyte files while installing Ubuntu. For reasons of performance, it's best if these are contiguous, rather than fragmented around the disk.

If you choose the repartitioning option to install Ubuntu, you may find that the Windows partition won't resize successfully if it is too fragmented. There's even a risk of data loss.

To defrag under Vista, open Computer on the Start menu, and right-click the hard disk icon. Select Properties and then the Tools tab in the dialog that appears. Click the DEFRAGMENT NOW button, and click the button with the same label in the dialog box that appears.

Under XP, open My Computer, right-click the hard disk icon, click Properties, then the Tools tab, and click the DEFRAGMENT NOW button. Click the DEFRAGMENT button in the program window that appears.

Checking the Windows filesystem for errors

It's a good idea to periodically check the Windows filesystem for errors under any circumstances, but it's vital if you opt to install Ubuntu by repartitioning the hard disk. If there are disk errors, repartitioning will fail. There's even a chance of data corruption.

To force a disk check in Windows XP, click Start ➪ Run, type cmd, and in the DOS window that appears, type chkdsk /f. Type Y when prompted, then reboot. Under Windows Vista, click the Start button, then type cmd into the Start Search text field. However, *don't* hit Enter! Instead type Ctrl+Shift+Enter. This will run the DOS window in privileged mode, and you'll be asked to authenticate. Once the DOS window appears, follow the steps as with Windows XP.

You should ensure Windows is shutdown cleanly before installing Ubuntu. If Windows crashes during shutdown, or you simply switch the power off, it won't be possible for Ubuntu to resize the partition.

Getting Ubuntu

Ubuntu is offered for download as an ISO image file. This is quite simply the contents of a CD-ROM in one large file. The ISO file is designed to be burned to a blank CD-R or CD-RW disk using your computer. Ubuntu can then be installed using this disc.

If you intend to use Wubi to install Ubuntu within the Windows filesystem, downloading the ISO image file is optional because Wubi can do it for you. See the *Within Windows (Wubi)* section later.

> **TIP** The Ubuntu install CD also includes a "live" mode that runs Ubuntu straight from the CD. This lets you try-out Ubuntu but it's too slow to be used permanently.

However, before downloading Ubuntu, you'll need to decide what version to use.

Choosing a version

The Ubuntu project has given rise to a number of spin-off projects. Each adapts the main Ubuntu release by adding and/or removing software, usually in the form of a different desktop environment, although some simply add-in specialist software.

> **NOTE** It's possible to switch to a different version of Ubuntu once it's been installed, so making this choice now is not critical.

Here are the main options:

Ubuntu main release: This is the standard version of Ubuntu. It's built around the user-friendly Gnome desktop environment (www.gnome.org) and includes a host of high-quality programs, including the Firefox web browser. If you don't know what version of Ubuntu to choose, this is the one for you.

> **NOTE** This book uses Ubuntu main release as a basis for all explanations, so is perhaps the best choice at this stage.

Kubuntu: This is a version of Ubuntu that uses the KDE desktop environment (www.kde.org) instead of Gnome. KDE is mostly

Table 1-1. Ubuntu derivatives.

Ubuntu version	Details
Edubuntu	Includes educational software and a child-friendly user-interface. Intended for use in educational environments. See www.edubuntu.org for more information.
Gobuntu	Adheres 100% to the Free Software Foundation principles, so doesn't include any proprietary or restrictively-trademarked software. For more information, see www.ubuntu.com/products/whatisubuntu/gobuntu. At the time of writing, this project is in limbo, and may be merged into the gNewSense project (http://gnewsense.org).
JeOS	Experimental release for server-based virtual appliances—see www.ubuntu.com/products/whatisubuntu/serveredition/jeos.
Ubuntu Server	For server hardware, such as web, mail and/or file servers. For more information, see www.ubuntu.com/products/whatisubuntu/serveredition.
Mobile and Embedded	Designed for handheld and ultra-portable devices—for more information, see www.ubuntu.com/products/mobile.
MythBuntu	Features the MythTV digital video recording software. For details of MythBuntu, see www.mythbuntu.org. For details of MythTV, see www.mythtv.org.
Ubuntu Studio	Includes multimedia editing and creation software. See http://ubuntustudio.org.

similar to Gnome but tends to offer more configuration options. It might be argued that Kubuntu is popular with power users. Kubuntu differs from Ubuntu in that it uses Konqueror for Web browsing and Kontact for email/PIM (although Firefox and other Ubuntu standard programs can be installed). There are a handful of other key differences too, particularly when it comes to system configuration tools, although the underlying system is still 100% Ubuntu.

NOTE Versions of Kubuntu prior to 8.04 used the older v3 series of KDE releases. 8.04 was released in both v3 and the newer experimental v4 series, but from 8.10 onwards, Kubuntu has standardized entirely on the v4 series.

Xubuntu: This version of Ubuntu is based on the Xfce desktop environment (www.xfce.org). This is a stripped-down desktop designed to run optimally on all types of hardware, particularly older, less-powerful computers. However, it features much of the same software as the main Ubuntu release, and is just as feature-packed. As with Kubuntu, it is still Ubuntu under the hood.

Others: Other projects make Ubuntu-derived releases. See Table 1-1 for a list of foremost examples. For more details, see https://wiki.ubuntu.com/DerivativeTeam/Derivatives/.

> **NOTE** Several third-parties use Ubuntu as a basis for their own versions of Linux. Examples include Linux Mint (www.linuxmint.com), that focuses on usability, and gNewSense (http://gnewsense.org), that strips out all software that isn't 100% Free Software (see the Gobuntu entry in Table 1-1).

Choosing a release

New releases of the main Ubuntu projects are made every six months. Every two years a *long-term support* (LTS) release is made.

Support

The chief difference between the LTS and ordinary releases is found in the length of time for which updates are provided. With a standard version of Ubuntu, software updates are provided for 18 months after release; upon expiry of this period, users are expected to upgrade to a newer release of Ubuntu. With an LTS version, *three years* of updates are provided before it becomes necessary to upgrade.

> **NOTE** On server hardware that uses the specialized Ubuntu Server release, five years of updates are provided.

Naming

Each Ubuntu release is named in two ways. The official name is the year and month combined, separated by a period. The release made in April 2008 was named *8.04*, for example.

Releases also have nicknames, decided upon by Mark Shuttleworth, and humorously derived from types of animals. 8.04 has the nickname *Hardy Heron*. 8.10 is called *Intrepid Ibex*. Sometimes the animal component is dropped in formal conversation—8.04 might be referred to simply as "Ubuntu Hardy", or just "Hardy".

Table 1-2 shows Ubuntu version numbers and nicknames.

Table 1-2. Ubuntu releases and support expiry dates.

Version number	Nickname	Updated until
4.10	Warty Warthog	April 2006
5.04	Hoary Hedgehog	October 2006
5.10	Breezy Badger	April 2007
6.06 LTS [1]	Dapper Drake	June 2009
6.10	Edgy Eft	April 2008
7.04	Feisty Fawn	October 2008
7.10	Gutsy Gibbon	April 2009
8.04 LTS	Hardy Heron	April 2011
8.10	Intrepid Ibex	April 2010
9.04	Jaunty Jackalope	October 2010

[1] 6.06 LTS was released eight months after the previous release, rather than six.

Making the best choice

What should you use? At the time of writing, the choice is either the 8.04LTS release, released April 2008, or the newer 8.10 release, released October 2008. There's no point using an earlier release than this because its support period will soon expire, if it hasn't already.

NOTE   Releases prior to 8.04 don't include the Wubi software.

8.04LTS offers support for a longer period, and is designed to be stable and reliable, so is the logical choice. Non-LTS releases are used to experiment with new features and software, so can be unpredictable and even buggy.

If you simply want to switch to Ubuntu for a fuss-free life then, undoubtedly, 8.04LTS is best. It's also ideal for corporate or home office environments. It is supported with updates until April 2011.

However, if you'd like to use cutting-edge software, and really see what the world of Linux has to offer right now, you might choose the 8.10 release. It is supported until April 2010.

NOTE   The 8.10 release also has much better wireless network and Bluetooth support than 8.04.

Downloading Ubuntu

To download Ubuntu, simply head off to www.ubuntu.com and click the relevant link to download the ISO image of Ubuntu.

Select the desktop edition for 32-bit computers.

NOTE You might notice that a 64-bit version of Ubuntu is also available for download. In my opinion, there's no need to use this, even if you have a 64-bit-capable CPU in your computer, *unless* your computer has more than 4GB of RAM. The 64-bit version of Ubuntu has been known to present a handful of annoying compatibility issues that, while not show-stoppers, can make life more difficult than it needs to be.

Remember: if you intend to use Wubi, you don't have to do this because Wubi can grab the Ubuntu installation files for you—see *Within Windows (Wubi)* section later in this chapter.

Alternatively, instead of burning a CD, you can have a CD of Ubuntu sent to you free-of-charge by using Ubuntu's Ship-It service. Just visit https://shipit.ubuntu.com and enter your mailing address.

TIP In fact, you can order a number of CDs thought Ship-It. This is ideal if you want to evangelize about Ubuntu and give copies to friends. Professionally-produced CDs always have more impact than a disc you've created yourself!

The Ship-It CD might take up to 10 weeks to reach you, however. For faster delivery, you might choose to buy a CD from the official Ubuntu shop: https://shop.canonical.com. Ubuntu CDs are also sold by a variety of retailers, including Amazon.com.

NOTE An Ubuntu DVD-ROM is also available. This contains all the available software for Ubuntu (thousands of programs!). However, in most cases the DVD is not necessary because all Ubuntu software is just a download away and most is rapidly updated after release, making the DVD go out of date quickly.

Creating an install CD

Assuming the download of the ISO image has finished, the next step is to burn it to disc, as follows:

NOTE If you intend to use the "virtual computer" method of trialing Ubuntu, there's no need to burn a CD. Instead, skip to the *Virtual Computer* heading on page 15.

1. You'll need a computer that has either a CD-R/RW or DVD-R/RW drive, a blank CD-R or CD-RW disc, and your Windows setup will need to have disc burning software installed. Applications like Nero can burn ISO file images, but if you haven't got it, head off to http://isorecorder.alexfeinman.com and download ISO Recorder. This freeware Windows application burns CD/DVD ISO images. You'll need to download

V2 if you have Windows XP, or V3 if you have Windows Vista. You will need the 32-bit version in each case, unless you know for sure that you're using a 64-bit version of Windows.

2. Once ISO Recorder has downloaded, install it and reboot.

3. When the desktop reappears, insert the blank CD-R or CD-RW disk. Right-click the Ubuntu ISO image file and select Copy Image To CD on the menu that appears (cancel any Windows dialog boxes that pop-up asking what you want to do with the blank CD-R/RW). ISO Recorder will start.

4. If you're using Windows Vista, click the Recording Speed dropdown list in the ISO Recorder interface and select the slowest speed possible. If you're running XP, in the ISO Recorder interface click the PROPERTIES button. Then click and drag the Recording Speed slider to the left, so it's at the lowest speed possible. Selecting a slow speed is necessary because burning ISO images to CD will fail if a high writing speed is used.

5. Click OK to close the dialog, and click the NEXT button to actually burn the disk.

The disc will be ejected when the burn has finished. Insert the disc again and skip to the relevant heading below that describes the installation method you wish to use.

Step-by-step: Installing Ubuntu

Three methods of installing Ubuntu are detailed below.

Standard (repartitioning)

This method of installing Ubuntu involves booting your computer using the Ubuntu CD and shrinking the Windows partition during installation to make space for Ubuntu.

> **NOTE** On a technical level, what happens is that the Windows partition is shrunk, and an extended partition created for Ubuntu. Following this, two new partitions are created inside the extended partition: *root*, that will contain the Ubuntu installation, and *swap*. The latter is like Windows' paging file, except it is contained in its own partition. Some Linux distros create separate partitions for operating system files and user data, but Ubuntu uses just one partition for all data.

The steps are as follows:

1. Insert the Ubuntu CD and reboot your computer. At the BIOS startup screen, look for the keypress option that brings up the boot device menu. Exactly what this is varies from computer to computer. On many computers you'll need to hit the Esc key, or F12. Select the CD/DVD-ROM drive from the menu when it appears. If there's no option for bringing up the boot device menu, enter BIOS setup by hitting the relevant key (usually Delete). Then configure the CD/DVD-ROM drive as the first boot device. Again, how this is done varies from PC to PC.

2. When the computer boots from the CD, the Ubuntu CD-ROM boot menu will appear. Using the up/down cursor keys, select your preferred language from the list and hit Enter. Then highlight the Install Ubuntu option on the main menu using the cursor keys and hit Enter.

3. Eventually the Ubuntu installation program window will appear, as shown in Figure 1-1. Work your way through the choices, such as entering your location and language choices, clicking the FORWARD button to move on each time.

4. After some time, the disk repartitioning choices will appear. Three options are listed: *Guided—Resize SCSI1 (0,0,0) Partition*; *Guided—Use Entire Disk*; and *Manual* (you may see *Guided—Resize IDE* instead of the first option, but it's the same thing). Guided—Resize Partition is the default choice, and the installer will attempt to choose the optimal resizing option for the Windows partition. A preview of the changes will be displayed in graphical form. By clicking and dragging the handle in the preview display alongside the New Partition Size heading, you can alter the size of the free space created (see Figure 1-2 overleaf, where the handle is indicated via an annotation; note that Figure 1-2 shows the Ubuntu 8.10 installer).

No changes are made until you click the FORWARD button. Usually the installer's default resizing choice is fine, but it can be a little aggressive in taking space for Ubuntu, so you might opt to drag the slider to preserve a little more free space in the Windows partition. If after clicking the FORWARD button you see the error message "Too small size", you will have to drag the slider a little to the right to give Windows more free space.

If you want to dedicate your computer's hard disk entirely to Ubuntu, and erase Windows , click the Guided—Use

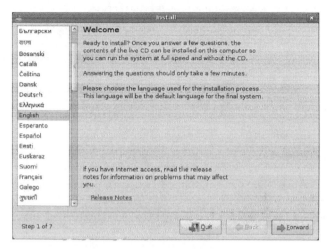

Figure 1-1. The Ubuntu installer.

Entire Disk option. You will need to select this option if installing Ubuntu on a second hard disk in your computer, in which case you should select the second entry in the list under the Guided—Use Entire Disk heading (probably identified as SCSI1 (0,0,1) sdb, but you can also use the size of the hard disk as a means of identifying it).

CAUTION If you opt to remove the Windows partition, be aware that there's no way of bringing it back. Be absolutely sure it's what you want to do.

The Manual option is for experts and lets you appropriate existing partitions (useful if you're upgrading from an older Ubuntu installation), or create new ones manually.

5. After making your partitioning choices, click FORWARD. You'll be asked to confirm your choices. Once repartitioning has finished, you'll be invited to create a user account. As directed, you'll need to type your chosen password twice to confirm correct typing.

TIP The password can contain numbers, letters, symbols, and even spaces. The longer and more complex a password, the stronger it is.

You'll also be invited to type a name for the computer. This is how your Ubuntu computer will be identified on a network. It's

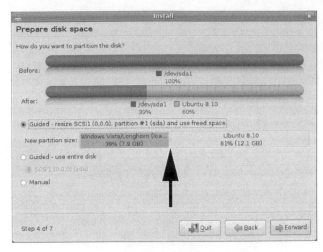

Figure 1-2. Resizing the Windows partition.

also the name that you'll see at the command prompt (as explained in Chapter 5). Ubuntu will make a suggestion based on your login name, but you can change it if you wish. Something like desktop-pc or laptop will be fine. Note that spaces and most symbols aren't allowed in the computer name.

If installing Ubuntu 8.10, you'll also see a Log In Automatically checkbox. If checked, Ubuntu will go straight to the desktop each time after booting, without prompting for a username/password.

CAUTION This option is considered highly insecure by some, but if you're sure only you will ever access your computer, you might opt to select it. Laptop owners should definitely think twice because it will mean any files are freely available to a thief should the computer get stolen.

6. Next, and assuming you haven't opted to wipe Windows, you're asked if you want to import Windows documents. All user accounts available under Windows will be shown, and you can put a check against any to automatically import into Ubuntu documents, wallpaper, and browser favorites.

7. Following this, you're presented with a summary. Click the INSTALL button and installation will commence. At this point you can relax. Installation will take up to half an hour. Once it's completed, you can progress to the next chapter.

Within Windows (Wubi)

Wubi allows Ubuntu to be installed inside Windows as a series of virtual hard disk files. It is perhaps the simplest and most fuss-free method of installing Ubuntu.

There are two methods of using Wubi:

1. Downloading the Wubi standalone installer and letting it download the Ubuntu installation files as needed during installation;

2. Inserting the Ubuntu installation CD while Windows is running and running Wubi from the CD.

There's no real benefit of one method over the other and, when it comes to the installation process, each is practically identical.

Here are the steps required whatever you choose:

1. If you would like to download the Wubi standalone program, and didn't create a CD earlier, head off to http://wubi-installer.org and click the Download Now link. Run the program once it's downloaded and skip to Step 3 below.

2. If you created an Ubuntu CD from the downloaded ISO image file, insert the Ubuntu CD while Windows is up and running. Select the Run Umenu.exe option, if prompted, and, from the menu that appears, select the Install Inside Windows option.

3. The Wubi program window will appear, as shown in Figure 1-3. Under the Installation Drive heading, select the partition or hard disk on which you want to place the Ubuntu files. Usually the default choice of C: is fine.

4. Under the Installation Size heading, choose how much space you'd like the Ubuntu installation to take-up. The default setting will probably be fine, but you can reduce it if disk space is tight.

5. If you're installing using the Ubuntu CD, there will be only one choice under the Desktop Environment heading, so leave this as it is. If you're using the standalone installer, here you can choose whether to install Ubuntu, Kubuntu, Xubuntu, or MythBuntu.

6. Under the Language heading, select your preferred language.

Figure 1-3. Installing Ubuntu inside Windows.

7. In the username text field, type a username you want to use within Ubuntu. Wubi will suggest a username based on your Windows login details, but you can type something different.

8. In the password fields, type the password you'd like to use for your Ubuntu login account. A good password involves letters, numbers, symbols and even spaces, and is as long as possible.

9. Once done, click the INSTALL button. There are two stages to the installation. First, the container files are created within the Windows filesystem (if you're using the standalone Wubi installer, the Ubuntu files are also downloaded; this may take some time). The computer then reboots for the full installation to take place. Upon rebooting, you should select Ubuntu from the boot menu—use the up/down cursor keys, and hit Enter when Ubuntu is highlighted.

Once installation has completed, you can boot into Ubuntu by selecting it each time at the boot menu.

Now skip to the next chapter to learn how to configure Ubuntu.

> **TIP** It's possible to convert a Wubi installation into a full hard disk installation. It's a little complicated, however, so you might like to try it when your skills improve. Instructions can be found at http://lubi.sourceforge.net/lvpm.html.

Virtual computer

A virtual computer is effectively an entire PC recreated in software. The virtual computer boots, just like a normal computer, and an operating system can be installed within it. The virtual computer's hard disk is contained within a file in the "host" filesystem. Once up and running, the "guest" operating system's desktop appears within a program window.

The free-of-charge VMware Player application allows easy virtual computing, and is ideal for trialing Ubuntu. Here are the steps required:

1. Head over to www.vmware.com/products/player and download VMware Player. Install it once downloaded. Then head over to www.ubuntupocketguide.com/vmware.html and download an empty virtual computer container zip file.

2. Extract the contents of the virtual computer zip into a new folder and copy the Ubuntu ISO image file you downloaded earlier into the same folder. Rename the ISO image as ubuntu.iso.

3. Start the virtual computer by double-clicking the startubuntu file in the new folder (you may see startubuntu.vmx, but it is the same file).

4. From this point onward, follow the instructions under the *Standard (Repartitioning)* heading above. When you come to the partitioning stage, you'll only see one option: Guided—Use Entire Disk. This is fine.

NOTE   Remember that you're installing Ubuntu onto a *virtual* hard disk, that is actually a file within your Windows filesystem. You aren't about to wipe the computer's real hard disk!

Once installation has finished, Ubuntu will "reboot" within the virtual computer—you don't have to reboot the real computer! When you've finished using Ubuntu, just quit VMware like you would any other program—the virtual Ubuntu installation will be suspended until you next start VMware by double-clicking the startubuntu file again.

Note that you'll need to click the mouse in the VMware window to switch keyboard and mouse input into the virtual operating system. Once this happens, the mouse cursor will be "locked" within the window. To free it, hit the Ctrl+Alt keys together.

Problematic installations (alternate install)

Sometimes Ubuntu's installation program goes wrong. Most commonly, this results in graphical problems that mean the installer program doesn't work correctly.

In situations such as this, you can use the *alternate install* CD. This can be downloaded from www.ubuntu.com as an ISO image, just like the main install CD (click the link marked "Text-based alternate installer installation disk", and, after selecting a download location near you, choose the file whose name ends with -alternate-i386.iso).

The alternate CD provides the same version of Ubuntu as the main install disc, but uses a "text mode" installer that doesn't have a graphical interface. As such the installer is compatible with virtually all computers, but this comes at a price because it isn't as user-friendly as the main Ubuntu installer. The terminology can be obtuse for beginners, and the lack of a graphical interface means no mouse—you must navigate around the interface using the keyboard.

Here are the steps needed to use the alternate install CD:

1. Assuming that you've downloaded the CD and burned it to a blank CD-R/RW disc, as described earlier, boot your computer using the disc. Follow Step 1 under the *Standard (Repartitioning)* heading to ensure your computer boots from the CD-R/RW disc.

2. At the boot menu, choose your language and select the Install Ubuntu menu option.

3. When the installer starts, follow the initial installation steps by highlighting a choice on-screen using the cursor keys, and hitting Enter. In most cases, the default choices are fine. At one stage the installer will attempt to go online, and might report an error. Don't worry about this. If you're prompted for wireless network details, just select not to go online (select "Do not configure the network at this time").

4. Eventually you'll be prompted for a hostname. This is how the computer is referred to on the network. The default is fine.

5. As with the main installer, the alternate installer will attempt to resize the Windows partition. Hit Enter when offered the Guided—Resize SCSI1 option (or Guided—Resize IDE1).

NOTE At this stage I saw a warning that "previous changes have to be written to the disk", even though I hadn't made any. Highlighting YES and hitting Enter allowed installation to continue.

6. Following this, you'll be invited to type a new size for the Windows partition. You'll be told the maximum and minimum possible sizes. By default, the alternate installer suggests taking the available free space in the Windows partition and splitting it equally in two, resizing the windows partition accordingly (in other words, Windows retains 50% of the free space, and 50% is made available for Ubuntu). This is often the best choice, and in most cases you can just hit Enter to continue. Repartitioning takes place immediately, so be sure of your choices before continuing. Once resizing has completed, you'll be invited to create the new partitions. Just highlight YES and hit Enter.

7. The Ubuntu installation procedure will now begin in earnest. Installation will pause when you're prompted to create a new login account. Simply answer the questions when prompted.

8. If you're installing Ubuntu 8.10, you will be asked if you want to create an encrypted /private folder. This is explained in more detail in Chapter 7. It's a good idea, so highlight YES and hit Enter. Following this you'll be prompted to create a passphrase, so do so (alternatively, just hit Enter to automatically create a random passphrase). Ensure you write down the passphrase.

9. When installation has finished, you'll be prompted to install the GRUB boot loader. Select YES and hit Enter. Once this is done, reboot the computer when prompted.

Progress to the next chapter to learn how to configure your system.

Getting Ubuntu onto an Apple Mac

You can use Ubuntu's install CD to install Ubuntu on Macs that use Intel CPUs. This will let you dual-boot Mac OS X and Ubuntu. However, you will first need to use OS X's Boot Camp feature to create space.

Instructions are below. These steps assume Windows is not installed on the Mac alongside OS X—complications are introduced if this is the case; see https://help.ubuntu.com/community/MacBook.

1. Start Boot Camp Assistant and follow the wizard as if to create a Windows installation. Boot Camp Assistant can be found by

opening Finder and clicking Applications, then selecting the Utilities folder. The Windows partition size you choose will equate to the Ubuntu partition size, so ensure more than 5GB is freed-up. When Boot Camp Assistant finishes shrinking the Windows partition, hit the QUIT & INSTALL LATER button.

2. You must now delete the NTFS (Windows) partition created by Boot Camp Assistant. To do this, open Disk Utility (as previously, it can be found in the Utilities folder). In the program window that appears, select the topmost entry in the list of disks on the left representing your hard disk, and click the PARTITION button on the right. Select the BOOTCAMP entry in the graphical preview of partitions, and click the minus button beneath. Then click REMOVE. When done, close Disk Utility.

3. Download and install the rEFIt software. This provides a boot menu that lets you choose between Mac OS X and Ubuntu. rEFIt can be downloaded from http://refit.sourceforge.net— choose the Mac disk image download. Note that there is no immediate sign that rEFIt is installed; it doesn't feature a configuration program within Applications, for example.

4. Insert the Ubuntu install CD and reboot your computer. Upon hearing the boot chime, hold down the C key. Eventually, you'll see the Ubuntu install disc boot menu. Follow the instructions on page 9 describing how to install Ubuntu. However, when the partitioning stage begins, don't resize. Instead, select Guided-Use the Largest Continuous Free Space.

NOTE There is a bug with Ubuntu 8.10 whereby selecting the Guided-Use the Largest Continuous Free Space option shows Ubuntu occupying the entire disk in the "After" graphical preview. This is incorrect and can be ignored.

5. Follow through the installation stages, as if installing on a standard PC. When you reboot, select the Linux penguin on the rEFIt boot menu to boot Ubuntu, or the Apple icon to boot OS X (use the cursor keys to highlight either, and hit Enter to select).

NOTE On my first boot after installation I found the rEFIt menu wasn't visible. After rebooting again, it appeared.

Users of older PowerPC Mac computers can download and install the community-supported PowerPC release of Ubuntu, although the installation is more complex because you must repartition manually. See https://wiki.ubuntu.com/PowerPC.

CHAPTER TWO

Configuring Ubuntu

In this chapter, you'll learn how to configure your new Ubuntu system. Every major area of hardware is tackled, including:

- Keyboard and mouse;
- Graphics and display(s);
- Sound;
- Networking (including wireless);
- Printing;
- Digital cameras/MP3 players/USB memory sticks;
- Flatbed scanners;
- Bluetooth devices.

Getting started

Put simply, Ubuntu just works. Unlike with Windows, you don't have to fiddle around with driver CDs after installation—support for all types of hardware is built into the central kernel program.

> **NOTE** The kernel is frequently updated, and each update brings better and better hardware support. This is one reason why you should keep your system updated. I explain how in Chapter 7.

However, you will still have to configure the system to your requirements—configuring Ubuntu to access your wireless network, for example, or setting-up the printer for optimal output.

Keyboard and mouse/trackpad

Entries for configuring the keyboard and mouse (or laptop trackpad) can be found on the System ⇨ Preferences menu—click the Keyboard entry and not the Keyboard Shortcuts entry to configure the keyboard.

The options presented shouldn't present any challenges to anybody who has configured a mouse or keyboard under Windows.

Switching keyboard languages

It's possible to switch between two or more keyboard layouts on the fly. This can be useful if you find yourself regularly typing in different languages. To configure this feature, follow these steps:

1. Open the Keyboard Preferences dialog (System ⇨ Preferences ⇨ Keyboard), and, ensuring the Layouts tab is selected, click the large plus button (click the +ADD button if using Ubuntu 8.04).

2. Select the keyboard layout from the Country/Variants dropdown lists. When you've made a selection, click the +ADD button.

3. In the parent dialog box, and in the list under the Selected Layouts heading, click the radio button alongside the entry you'd like to be default. This will be the layout activated when Ubuntu boots. When done, click the CLOSE button.

4. Right-click the bar running across the top of the screen, and select Add to Panel in the menu that appears. In the dialog that appears, click and drag the Keyboard Indicator entry to a panel. Then click CLOSE.

From now on you can switch between layouts by clicking the applet—clicking will cycle through the choices of keyboard layout you selected in the Keyboard Preferences dialog.

Mouse

If the pointer seems to move too quickly for you, open the Mouse Preferences dialog box (System ⇨ Preferences ⇨ Mouse), and click and drag the Acceleration slider a little to the left. Changes take effect immediately, so test the mouse movement and adjust again if necessary until you're entirely happy with the settings.

To deactivate touchpad tap-to-click, so that only clicking a touchpad's mouse button performs a left click, select the Touchpad tab and remove the check from the relevant box.

Graphics

In nearly all cases Ubuntu's graphical subsystem will work fine straight away. However, there are a handful of common but easily fixed issues.

Changing screen resolution

Ubuntu might guess the wrong screen resolution after installation. You'll know if this is the case because everything will appear blocky and/or blurred. To adjust the resolution, click the System menu at the top of the screen, and then Preferences ➪ Screen Resolution.

> **NOTE** You may have to adjust the Refresh Rate dropdown if you're using a CRT monitor (i.e. a glass tube display, rather than a TFT LCD panel). The standard refresh rate most find comfortable is 75Hz. Flat panels should be set to 60Hz.

If the screen resolution you want isn't available in the Resolution dropdown list, or just doesn't work when selected, you might have to activate the proprietary graphics card drivers, as described below.

Installing proprietary drivers

Installing proprietary graphics card drivers means Ubuntu will no longer use the Free Software versions. It should only be done if absolutely necessary (for example, if the built-in drivers don't produce optimal results) because proprietary drivers are not updated as frequently as the Free Software versions and, some suggest, can be very buggy.

To install proprietary drivers, first ensure you're online—see the *Getting Online* section later. This is necessary because the new drivers will be downloaded. Then click System ➪ Administration ➪ Hardware Drivers.

If you're using Ubuntu 8.10, select the entry in the list for your graphics driver and click the ACTIVATE button (see Figure 2-1 for an example).

> **TIP** If several drivers are offered, select the one that's marked "Recommended". If this proves less than optimal, repeat this step and choose a different version.

If you're using Ubuntu 8.04, simply put a check in the Enabled column alongside the entry for your graphics card.

With either version of Ubuntu, the new graphics driver will be downloaded once you've made the selection. You may have to reboot the computer once it's finished installing—just follow the on-screen prompts.

Figure 2-1. Utilizing proprietary graphics drivers.

Activating desktop visual effects

As with all modern operating systems, Ubuntu includes a number of desktop visual effects that mean program windows fade into view when first activated, or visually shrink when minimized. This can make using Ubuntu a much more pleasant experience.

Visual effects are made possible through the use of advanced graphics drivers. On systems utilizing some Intel or AMD/ATI graphics chips, open source versions of such drivers are available and will be installed by default, but for computers utilizing certain graphics chipsets, proprietary drivers must be installed for desktop effects to work.

You can tell if your computer has desktop effects already activated by holding down Ctrl+Alt and hitting the left or right arrow keys. This will activate virtual desktop switching (I explain more about this in Chapter 3). If the desktop "slides" out of view, visual effects are already activated and no further work is needed. If you see a small panel appear in the middle of the screen showing the virtual desktops, then visual effects are not activated, and you might choose to utilize proprietary graphics drivers by following the steps mentioned under the *Installing Proprietary Drivers* heading above.

NOTE Desktop visual effects aren't an absolute necessity—Ubuntu is fully functional without them, even if it's less pretty.

To control the types of visual effects in use, or to deactivate them, click System ➪ Preferences ➪ Appearance. In the program window that appears, select the Visual Effects tab and select either None, Normal or Extra. The Normal setting is default.

TIP For even more control over visual effects, install the compiz-config-settings-manager software package. I explain more about software installation in Chapter 6.

Configuring a second monitor

If you have more than one display device attached, Ubuntu will mirror the contents of the desktop across them, and choose the higher of the two output device resolutions as the desktop resolution. This can be handy if you have an LCD projector attached for presentations, but not so useful if you have two monitors attached to your computer.

To switch to an expanded desktop across the two display devices, so that each monitor gets its own separate desktop area, click System ➪ Preferences ➪ Screen Resolution, and, in the dialog box that appears, ensure there's not a check alongside the Mirror Screens/Clone Screens heading. Then click and drag the icon for the second display to where you'd like it to be "placed" in relation to the main monitor (i.e. to the left, right, or even above or below). This will affect where the cursor has to be moved to leave one desktop and enter the other on the second monitor.

TIP On one of my test systems, the icon for the second screen appeared to be "hidden behind" the first screen. Clicking the first screen's icon revealed it!

By selecting the icon for each display device in the preview, you can also set the resolution you'd like that display to use in the Resolution drop-down list.

Once done, click the APPLY button. If the two monitors have different resolutions, you'll be asked if you want the virtual resolution to be set to match the screen resolution. This is fine, so click the YES button.

Agree to save your changes, if prompted. You will have to log out and back in again (System ⇨ Log Out in Ubuntu 8.10; System ⇨ Quit in Ubuntu 8.04) for the changes to take effect.

> **TIP** If you find the graphical settings get scrambled while config-uring multiple monitors, reboot your computer and, at the boot menu, choose the Ubuntu "recovery mode" option (usually the second choice in the list). When a second menu appears, select the xfix option. Then select the resume option to boot normally.

Changing screen backlighting

If you're using Ubuntu on a notebook computer, you should be able to alter the screen backlighting brightness using the notebook's standard keyboard combination, as with Windows. If this doesn't work, right-click a blank spot on the bar running across the top of the screen and select Add to Panel from the menu that appears. In the list that appears, select Brightness Applet and click the ADD button. This will add a new icon that, when clicked, presents a slider that will let you alter the degree of backlighting.

Screensaver

You can choose a screensaver and adjust the amount of time after which it activates by clicking System ⇨ Preferences ⇨ Screensaver.

Sound

You can change the audio volume by clicking the speaker icon at the top-right of the desktop. Double-clicking this icon will bring up the main mixer window where you can control the volume of individual components of the sound system, such as the CD player, or PCM (PCM is the audio output from applications, including media players and the web browser).

> **NOTE** PCM is sometimes referred to as "wave" or "wav" under Windows.

To fully exploit the feature set of your sound card, click the PREFERENCES button in the main mixer window and put a check alongside any controls you'd like to add to the main mixer window (in Ubuntu 8.04, click Edit ⇨ Preferences). The new slider or control will be added immediately.

The precise features offered will depend on the capabilities of your com-puter's sound hardware. For example, to add a slider control for surround sound, put a check alongside the relevant checkbox in the list.

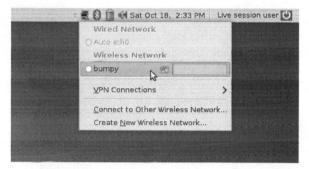

Figure 2-2. Connecting to a wireless network.

Getting online

Depending on the hardware used, there are a variety of ways of getting online and/or connecting to a network. I deal with each separately below.

Wireless

Network connections are handled by Ubuntu's NetworkManager applet that can be found at the top right of the desktop. Its icon is two monitors inset against each other. Clicking it will show a list of nearby wireless networks, as shown in Figure 2-2. Connecting to a network is simply a matter of selecting it and typing the wireless password when prompted. When done, click CONNECT.

> **TIP** Ensure the right kind of wireless protection (i.e. WEP/WPA) has been detected by Ubuntu. Ubuntu got this wrong in one of my tests. You can select by clicking the Wireless Security dropdown.

To connect to a wireless network that doesn't broadcast its name (ESSID), click the NetworkManager icon and select Connect to Hidden Wireless Network from the menu (or Connect to Other Wireless Network under Ubuntu 8.04). Type the ESSID into the Network Name text field, and select the correct type of wireless protection from the Wireless Security dropdown list, filling-in the appropriate key/ passphrase details beneath this. Click the CONNECT button when done.

The Ubuntu 8.10 release includes much better wireless hardware support than earlier releases. If you find your wireless hardware isn't supported by Ubuntu, and you're using Ubuntu 8.04 or earlier, consider upgrading. You'll know if the wireless card isn't supported because no wireless networks will be detected, although you should also ensure your computer's wireless function is activated—with some notebooks, a special key combination must be hit, or wireless networking specifically enabled in the computer's BIOS setup.

TIP If you're faced with non-working wireless, you might try installing the `linux-backports-modules-intrepid` package, if using Ubuntu 8.10, or `linux-backports-modules-hardy`, if using Ubuntu 8.04 (reboot after installing). If that doesn't fix it, you might consider using Ndiswrapper. This is a hardware driver that lets you use Windows wireless drivers under Linux. I wrote about Ndiswrapper in my book *Ubuntu Kung Fu*. You can read the relevant extract by visiting the *Ubuntu Kung Fu* website: www.ubuntukungfu.org/ndiswrapper.html.

Wired (Ethernet)

As soon as you attach an Ethernet cable to your computer, your computer will be online straight away. No configuration is necessary.

The exception is if your network doesn't automatically assign IP addresses (i.e. it lacks a DHCP server). This is rare, but is sometimes the case in certain workplaces. In this case you'll need to enter the IP, subnet mask, gateway, and DNS addresses manually, as follows.

Configuring a static IP address (Ubuntu 8.10 and above)

To configure a static IP address (non-DHCP) under Ubuntu 8.10, right-click the NetworkManager icon at the top-right of the screen and select Edit Connections. In the window that appears, ensure the Wired tab is selected and click the Auto eth0 entry. Click the EDIT button. In the new window that appears, click the IPv4 Settings tab, and select Manual from the Method dropdown list. Click the ADD button and enter your IP address, subnet mask, and gateway (router) details by clicking the entries under relevant headings. Add the DNS addresses in the DNS Servers text field (separate each address by a comma). You can leave the Search Domains field blank. Click OK when done and reboot the computer.

Configuring a static IP address (Ubuntu 8.04)

To configure a static IP address under Ubuntu 8.04, click System ⇨ Administration ⇨ Network. In the program window that appears, click the UNLOCK button and enter your password when prompted. Select the Wired Connection entry and click the PROPERTIES button. In the dialog box that appears, uncheck Enable Roaming Mode and, in the

Configuration dropdown list, select Static IP Address. Enter the IP address, subnet mask, and gateway (router) details into the relevant text fields. Click OK and, in the parent dialog box, click the DNS tab and then the ADD button. Enter the first DNS address and hit Enter. Click ADD again and enter the second DNS address. Once done, click the CLOSE button. You may have to reboot your computer before the new configuration works.

Printers

Your printer will be automatically detected and configured by Ubuntu. You can check to see if your printer has been detected by clicking System ⇨ Administration ⇨ Printing. If you're using Ubuntu 8.10, the printer will be shown as an icon in the window that appears. With Ubuntu 8.04, the printer will be listed beneath the Local Printers heading on the left of the dialog box that appears.

> **TIP** Ensure your printer is turned on—it can't be detected by Ubuntu otherwise! It takes Ubuntu a few seconds to install and configure a printer after it's just been attached or first switched on. You'll be told when configuration has finished via a call-out balloon at the top right of the screen.

Printing a test page

To print a test page in Ubuntu 8.10, open the Printer Configuration window (System ⇨ Administration ⇨ Printing), then double-click the printer's icon and click the PRINT TEST PAGE button. In Ubuntu 8.04, open the Printer Configuration dialog as described previously, click the printer's entry in the list on the left, and click the PRINT TEST PAGE button (ensure the Settings tab is selected in the program window first).

Setting default print options

To set the default print options, such as paper type or print quality, open the Printer Configuration window (System ⇨ Administration ⇨ Printing) and, if you're using Ubuntu 8.10, double-click the printer's icon in the window that appears. Following this, click the Printer Options entry in the list on the left of the program window. In Ubuntu 8.04, open the Printer Configuration dialog as described previously and ensure the printer is selected on the left of the program window. Then click the Printer Options tab.

In either version, you can then select from the dropdown lists alongside each heading in the list. Once done, click the APPLY button and, if using Ubuntu 8.10, subsequently click OK to close the window.

Managing print jobs

To view or cancel print jobs, click Applications ⇨ Accessories ⇨ Manage Print Jobs. This will display the current print queue. To delete a job, right-click its entry in the list and select Cancel.

If a print job stalls for whatever reason, an icon will appear at the top-right of the screen. Double-clicking this will bring-up the printer queue window automatically.

Installing a network printer

To install a shared network printer in Ubuntu 8.10, such as one connected to another computer in your home or office, click System ⇨ Administration ⇨ Printing and click the NEW button in the toolbar (click NEW PRINTER if using Ubuntu 8.04). Then select the type of network printer you'd like to connect to across the network.

For printers utilizing a network server device—normally found only in corporate environments—select AppSocket/HP JetDirect. Enter the address details on the right of the program window. This will probably take the form of an IP address and a queue name—see your administrator for these, or the print server's documentation.

If connecting to a shared printer on a Windows PC, select Windows Printer via SAMBA, and click the BROWSE button to have Ubuntu automatically detect shared printers on the local network, as shown in Figure 2-3. Click the chevrons alongside each heading to "unfold" them and, when you find the printer you're looking for, select it and click the OK button.

Back in the parent window, click the radio button alongside Set Authentication Details Now (under Ubuntu 8.04 click the Authentication Required checkbox) and enter the *Windows* (not Ubuntu!) login username/password required to access the Windows account that's sharing the printer. Click VERIFY to check that the details work.

Click Forward when done to install the printer driver. It is unlikely it will be detected, and you will have to select it manually by working through the list of printer manufacturers and models.

> **TIP** You may have to adjust the firewall and/or sharing preferences on the Windows computer to be able to access the printer.

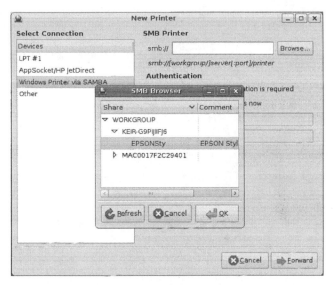

Figure 2-3. Connecting to a printer that's shared on a Windows PC.

Removable storage

Removable storage is an umbrella term describing any plug-in hardware that stores data. Examples include:

- USB memory sticks;
- External hard disks or CD/DVD-ROM drives;
- Digital cameras;
- Memory card readers (including those built-into a computer as well as those that attach by USB);
- Media players, such as iPods and other MP3 players.

All are accessed in a similar way under Ubuntu. Whenever you attach them, a file browsing window will appear automatically showing the contents of the device, and an icon will appear on the desktop; you can double-click this to reopen the file browsing window should you close it. Additionally, an entry will be added to the Places menu at the top of the screen, and selecting it will also let you browse the device.

NOTE If you attach a memory card reader, it won't appear to be connected until a memory card is actually inserted into it.

With some removable storage devices that have specific uses, such as digital cameras or MP3 players, the relevant Ubuntu application might also start; plug-in a digital camera and F-Spot Photo Manager will appear, for example. If you don't wish to use the application at that time, just click its close button.

> **TIP**   To change what applications start when certain types of removable storage devices are attached, or to stop them starting, open a file browsing window (click Places ⇨ Home Folder) and click Edit ⇨ Preferences on the file browser menu. Select the Media tab in the window that appears, and choose from the dropdown lists that appear.

There's an important difference when using removable storage devices in Ubuntu, when compared to Windows. Before physically removing the device from the USB socket, you must *unmount* it. This can be done by right-clicking the desktop icon and selecting either the Eject, Unmount, or Unmount Volume option (the terminology varies depending on context). Alternatively, in Ubuntu 8.10, you can click the eject icon next to the removable storage device's icon on the left of a file browsing window.

Once the device has been unmounted, and the LED light on it has ceased flashing, it can be physically removed from the computer.

> **NOTE**   Other USB devices, such as printers or Bluetooth dongles, can simply be pulled out at will—no unmounting necessary—although watch out for printers that have built-in card readers. If any cards are inserted, they will have to be unmounted first.

Scanners

Scanners are installed and configured for use automatically. Ubuntu includes some excellent scanning software in the form of XSane Image Scanner that can be found on the Applications ⇨ Graphics menu. This operates in a very similar way to Windows scanner drivers.

> **TIP**   If you want to utilize optical character recognition (OCR), install the gocr software package. Software installation is explained in Chapter 6. Once gocr is installed, you can start it by clicking File ⇨ OCR-Save as Text in the Xsane viewer window after scanning.

Bluetooth

If your computer has Bluetooth capabilities, a Bluetooth icon will appear at the top-right of the screen. This can be used to configure all aspects of Bluetooth connectivity.

Pairing (Ubuntu 8.10)

If you're using Ubuntu 8.10, and wish to pair your Ubuntu PC with a device, ensure what you want to connect to is set to be "discoverable" and click the Bluetooth icon on Ubuntu's desktop. Select Setup New Device from the menu that appears and click the FORWARD button in the dialog box. The device you want to pair with will instantly appear in the list of detected devices, although it might not immediately be identified by its make/model details. Just wait a second or two for the full information to appear. Select the device in the list and click the FORWARD button. You'll be given a PIN to enter on the device, so do so. Once this is done, the devices will be paired.

NOTE   On some Bluetooth devices you may have to further authorize the pairing. How this is done varies according to device.

Pairing (Ubuntu 8.04)

Bluetooth functionality under Ubuntu 8.04 is less than perfect. If you intend to use Bluetooth devices with Ubuntu frequently, I recommend upgrading to Ubuntu 8.10. However, if you have no other choice, the following instructions should suffice.

First, right-click the Bluetooth icon and select Preferences from the menu that appears. In the dialog box that appears, ensure the first tab is selected (the tab's title will relate to the name of your Ubuntu system), and click Visible and Connectable for Other Devices.

Initiate pairing on the Bluetooth device. How this is done varies from device to device but once it's done a callout will appear at the top-right of the Ubuntu desktop prompting you to type the PIN you entered on the device. Once this is done, the devices will be paired.

TIP   Be quick when you're pairing devices—the time period during which the PIN can be entered on the other device is a matter of seconds before pairing will be automatically cancelled.

Transferring files

Once a device has been paired to Ubuntu, you can send files between the two (assuming the file is capable of file transfer; examples include mobile phones or even other computers).

Sending a file from Ubuntu

To send a file from an Ubuntu computer, right-click the file and select Send To in the menu that appears. Ensure Bluetooth (OBEX Push) is selected in the Send As dropdown list, and the paired device is selected in the Send To dropdown list. Finally, click the SEND button.

Sending a file to Ubuntu

Right-click the Bluetooth icon and select Preferences in the menu that appears. In the dialog box, ensure the first tab is selected and click the Temporary Visible entry (this is referred to as Limited Discoverable and Connectable under Ubuntu 8.04). Initiate file transfer on the Bluetooth device, and respond to the prompts that appear on the Ubuntu desktop.

CHAPTER THREE

Getting to grips with the desktop

This chapter describes the highways and byways of the Ubuntu desktop—the component of Ubuntu that you'll be spending most time with. It also describes a handful of common administrative tasks that you might want to undertake. Topics covered include:

- Logging into the system for the first time;
- Understanding what's what on the desktop;
- Working with virtual desktops;
- Customizing Ubuntu's look and feel;
- The most useful day-to-day applications;
- Using the clipboard (cutting, copying and pasting);
- Searching for files (including the desktop search feature);
- Adding new users to the system;
- Rebooting, suspending, and switching off the computer.

Logging in

Let's start from the very beginning—turning-on your computer (or rebooting) for the first time after installation.

The first thing you'll see, after the computer has finished its self-testing, is a boot menu. This lets you choose between Ubuntu and Windows.

Wubi (Windows install)

If you used Wubi to install Ubuntu, you'll see just two choices—Windows, and Ubuntu. Use the up/down cursor keys to make your selection and hit Enter once you've done so.

This boot menu is actually provided by Windows. If you choose the Ubuntu option, you'll start the Ubuntu boot process, and if you hit a key during the on-screen countdown, you can access Ubuntu's *own* boot menu. Day-to-day there's no reason to do this, although it offers a useful recovery option for fixing problems.

Dual-boot

If you installed Ubuntu in the traditional repartitioning way, after your PC's power-on self-tests you'll move straight to the Ubuntu boot menu. This has a more involved list of options.

At the top of the menu are always two options relating to Ubuntu. The first boots Ubuntu in normal mode, while the second starts recovery mode—Ubuntu's equivalent of Windows' "safe mode", where system repairs can be carried out.

The third menu option starts a memory testing program that is separate from Ubuntu, and can be useful for diagnosing hardware faults.

> **TIP** For more information on this program, see www.memtest.org.

Windows occupies the bottom position in the list and you can move the selection highlight between options using the up/down cursor keys. Hit Enter to confirm your choice and start the boot procedure.

> **NOTE** If you wiped Windows during installation, the boot menu won't appear unless you hit a key during the on-screen countdown.

If you didn't select the automatic login option during installation, the next thing you will see, after Ubuntu has finished the first stage of booting, is the login screen. See Figure 3-1 for an example.

Simply type your username, hit Enter, and type your password. Assuming both details are correct, booting will finish, and the desktop will appear.

> **TIP** If you want Ubuntu to login automatically on future boot-ups, as with some versions of Windows, click System ⇨ Administration ⇨ Login Window. Type your login password when prompted. In the dialog box that appears, click the Security tab. Put a check in the Enable Automatic Login box, and select your username from the User dropdown list. Click the CLOSE button when done.

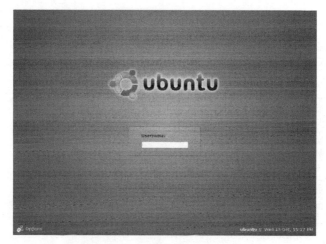

Figure 3-1. The Ubuntu 8.10 login screen.

The layout of the desktop

The Ubuntu desktop might seem a little strange at first, but don't worry. You'll soon get used to it.

Panels

The Ubuntu desktop differs from Windows in that it has two taskbars (known within Ubuntu as *panels*)—one at the top of the screen, and one at the bottom.

The one at the top is concerned with presenting information, starting programs, and configuring the system. The panel at the bottom is where programs minimize to, and this panel also includes a Show Desktop button (left), a trash icon (right), and a virtual desktop selector (right; of which more later). Files can be dragged and dropped onto the trash icon, and clicking it lets you view and empty the trash contents.

Main menus

The three menus at the top of the screen (Applications, Places, System) are known as the *main menus*. They stay on-screen all the time. When an application starts, its own menus appear within its program window beneath.

The Applications menu at the top left provides access to GUI software installed on the system.

The Places menu, alongside it, offers quick access to locations within the filesystem, or attached storage such as USB memory sticks. Digital cameras and MP3 players are also listed here when plugged-in.

NOTE I go into more detail about the Ubuntu filesystem in Chapter 4, and also explain the file manager in detail.

The System menu, alongside the Places menu, offers control over your computer's settings. It has two submenus, as follows:

Preferences: This menu mostly lets you tweak settings relating to your particular user account and the operation of the desktop. You can also alter some hardware settings, such as the screen resolution, but only those that relate to your personal desktop configuration.

Administration: This menu offers system-wide hardware configuration options, such as altering the time/date, and options for configuring the underlying Ubuntu system, such as adding/removing software.

Icons and applets

Alongside the menus are quick launch icons for the web browser, email client, and help system, respectively.

TIP You can add your own icons here by clicking and dragging them from the menus, or even from the desktop.

At the right of the top panel is a time/date display, along with a system tray area (known within Ubuntu as the *notification area*). As with Windows, various icons appear here informing you of the system status (such as battery charge if you're using a laptop), or when certain administrative actions are required. For example, as soon as you get online, you will notice the Update Manager icon appears, informing you that software updates are available. Clicking the icon will start the Update Manager program.

Each panel can house any number of *applets*—small programs with a specific function. Several are available. To add an applet, just right-click a blank spot on either panel, select Add to Panel from the list, and select from the list that appears. To subsequently remove an applet (or any existing item on a panel), right-click it and select Remove from Panel.

CAUTION Just about everything on either panel can be removed in this way, including the main menus! In fact, technically speaking, everything you see on the panels—including the main menus—are actually applets and, therefore, also appear in the applet list.

Virtual desktops

Like all Linuxes, Ubuntu makes use of virtual desktops. This handy function is missing from Windows although it can be found in Macintosh OS X 10.5 under the name of Spaces.

Using virtual desktops is like having a second (or third, or fourth etc.) monitor. Program windows can be placed on any of the desktops of the "monitors" and you can switch between desktops using the applet at the bottom-right of the screen.

TIP You can quickly switch between desktops by holding down Ctrl+Alt and hitting the left/right cursor keys. You can also switch by turning the mouse wheel when the mouse cursor is hovered over the virtual desktop applet.

Virtual desktops are best explained by example, so start a program of your choice (maybe the Firefox web browser) and switch to the second desktop by clicking the second of the screen icons in the virtual desktop applet at the bottom right of the screen. The program window will seem to disappear. Now open a file browsing window (click Places ⇨ Home Folder), and return to the first desktop by clicking the first of the screen icons. The first desktop's contents will now reappear.

See how it works? You could set aside one virtual desktop solely for email, and another for day-to-day tasks such as web browsing, and switch between the desktops when necessary.

You can have up to 36 virtual desktops—just right-click the icon, select Preferences, and increase the number in the Number of Workspaces counter. You can also give each a descriptive name in the Workspace Names section—just double-click an entry in the list and overtype.

TIP You can move a program window from one desktop to another by right-clicking the window's title bar and selecting Move to Workspace Right (or Left) from the menu that appears. If you have more than two virtual desktops, you can choose from a list of them on the submenu.

Personalizing

Just about any element of the Ubuntu user interface can be customized, from the desktop wallpaper to the program titlebars and buttons.

To view the personalization options, click System ⇨ Preferences ⇨ Appearance. This will open the Appearance Preferences dialog box, and you can select between the tabs in the program window to make your choices.

Themes

The look and feel of program windows and dialog boxes is known as a *theme*, and several are available within Ubuntu, above and beyond the orange default appearance. You can switch between them by selecting the Theme tab in the Appearance Preferences dialog box. Changes take effect immediately.

By clicking the CUSTOMIZE button, you can fine-tune personalization of program windows and dialog boxes, including changing the colors used. See Figure 3-2 for an example. As above, changes are applied the instant you make them.

> **TIP**   New themes and wallpaper can be downloaded from websites such as http://gnome-look.org. Once the new theme has downloaded, just drag and drop the archive file anywhere on the Appearance Preferences dialog box to install it. There's no need to unpack the archive first. Additionally, several community-generated themes can be added to Ubuntu 8.10 by installing the package community-themes, and some excellent wallpapers added by installing the gnome-backgrounds package (on both 8.10 and 8.04). Software installation is described in Chapter 6.

Fonts

Under Ubuntu it's not only possible to customize what fonts are used for various elements of the desktop display, but also fine-tune how they appear on screen (known as *font rendering*). To tweak font settings, click System ⇨ Preferences ⇨ Appearance and select the Fonts tab.

To change the font used for Applications, or the Desktop, and so on, click the dropdown list alongside each heading.

To change how fonts appear, choose an entry under the Rendering heading, or click the DETAILS button to get an even greater degree of control. If you're using an LCD panel or laptop computer, you will almost certainly want to select the Subpixel (LCD) option, although this is a matter of personal taste. Just play around until you're happy with the results.

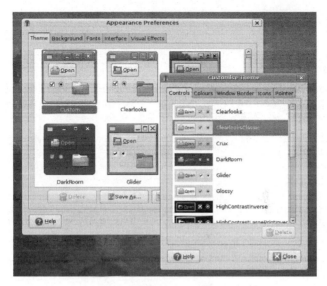

Figure 3-2. Customizing the desktop theme.

> **TIP** You can import your own fonts into Ubuntu by creating a new
> folder in your /home folder called .fonts (note the period at the
> start of fonts), and placing TrueType (.ttf) font files in it. Note
> that this is a hidden folder, and won't show up in normal file
> listings; to view it, click View ⇨ Show Hidden Files in a file brows-
> ing window. Once added, the new fonts will be instantly available
> in applications. A common trick is to copy fonts from Windows.

Login screen

To personalize the login screen that appears when you boot into
Ubuntu, click System ⇨ Administration ⇨ Login Window and, in
the dialog box that appears, click the Local tab. Then select from the list
of themes.

> **TIP** As with the desktop theme, new login screen themes can be
> downloaded from sites like http://gnome-look.org. New themes
> can also be found in Ubuntu's software repositories; they usually
> have the words gdm-theme somewhere in their package names.
> Software installation is described in Chapter 6.

Configuring menus

The contents of the Applications and System main menus can be
customized by selecting System ⇨ Preferences ⇨ Main Menu. Click and

drag to rearrange the order of menu items, or uncheck an item to remove it from the menu.

Customizing desktop icons

Icons are usually customized as part of the broader desktop theme, but you can use your own picture for a desktop icon by right-clicking it, selecting Properties, and clicking the top-left icon preview in the dialog box that appears. Following this, navigate to a picture file.

Any icon on the desktop can be resized by right-clicking it and selecting Stretch Icon. Drag the handles at the corners of the icon to resize.

Useful applications

There isn't space in a pocket guide such as this to run through commonly-used applications in detail. Nor is there any need because the applications are extremely intuitive and will present no problems to anybody who has used similar programs under Windows.

Table 3-1 overleaf shows a list of the applications most Ubuntu users use day-to-day, and provides an overview of their functionality, along with hints about how to initially configure them, if necessary.

Cutting, copying, and pasting

Ubuntu offers two separate methods of copying and pasting text.

The first is the standard way that you may be aware of, wherein text is first highlighted and either copied or cut by selecting the relevant entries on the program's Edit menu (or by tapping Ctrl+C or Ctrl+X). The text is then pasted into its new location by clicking Edit ⇨ Paste (or by hitting Ctrl+V).

The second method is independent of this, and unique to Linux/Unix. It uses the *selection buffer*. How it works is this: As soon as any text is highlighted, it is automatically copied into the selection buffer. It can then be pasted at the text cursor's position by clicking the *middle* mouse button. You might not think your mouse has one of these, but it does—on most mice, the scroll wheel acts as a middle mouse button.

> **TIP** On mice without a scroll wheel, you can click the left and right mouse buttons at exactly the same time, and this will emulate clicking the middle mouse button.

To give this a try, open the text editor (Applications ⇨ Accessories ⇨ Text Editor). Type something, highlight it using the mouse (or by holding down Shift and using the cursor keys), and click the middle mouse button. Whatever was highlighted will appear at the text cursor's position, as if you had just typed it. Note that this will only work as long as the selection remains highlighted.

Desktop search

Ubuntu offers a powerful desktop search tool in the form of Tracker. Unlike standard file searching tools, Tracker is able to catalog the *contents* of files such as PDFs or office documents, as well as their filenames. This means you are able to search not only by filename, but by key phrases that the document might contain.

To activate Tracker, click System ⇨ Preferences ⇨ Search and Indexing. Put a check in the Enable Indexing and Enable Watching boxes. If you're using a notebook computer, you might also check Disable All Indexing When on Battery. Click OK once done, and click the RESTART button when prompted.

NOTE Tracker isn't activated by default because of fears over battery life with laptop computers—Tracker has to frequently access the disk to build its index, and this consumes power. Some also have concerns about Tracker's effect on overall computer performance. The best bet is to give it a try. You can always turn it off if you don't like it.

Once Tracker is activated a new icon will be added to the notification area at the top-right of the screen. By clicking this, you will be able to type a search term, or word. Note that it will take a few moments for the initial search index to build after Tracker is activated.

TIP To have Tracker index the contents of Microsoft Word documents, install the wv package. Software installation is explained in Chapter 6. Once wv is installed, force Tracker to reindex by right-clicking the search icon and selecting the option from the menu that appears.

Deskbar

Although it might be considered an adjunct to Tracker, Ubuntu's Deskbar search applet is a separate tool with its own feature set. It can be added to a panel by right-clicking a blank spot on the panel, selecting Add to Panel from the menu that appears, selecting Deskbar in the applet list, and clicking the ADD TO PANEL button.

Table 3-1. Useful day-to-day Ubuntu applications.

Type	Application	Details
Web browser	Firefox *Applications* ⇨ *Internet* ⇨ *Firefox Web Browser*	Fully capable alternative to Internet Explorer for general browsing and accessing interactive "Web 2.0" applications, such as Google Docs (`http://docs.google.com`). Several add-ons can be installed to provide additional functionality, and the interface can be personalized—click Tools ⇨ Add-ons to do so.
Instant Messaging	Pidgin *Applications* ⇨ *Internet* ⇨ *Pidgin Internet Messenger*	Highly capable chat program that "speaks" AIM, Yahoo!, MSN, IRC, ICQ, and many other protocols. Upon starting it for the first time you'll be prompted to add an initial account. More accounts can be added subsequently (click Accounts ⇨ Manage Accounts), so you can chat to all your contacts through the same program.
Email/PIM	Evolution *Applications* ⇨ *Internet* ⇨ *Evolution Mail*	All-in-one email client, calendar application, contacts book, and organizer. It unashamedly borrows from Microsoft Outlook, and is perhaps one of the most powerful and businesslike tools in Ubuntu's armory. Upon starting you'll be walked-through configuring an initial email account.
Image editing & cataloging	GIMP *Applications* ⇨ *Graphics* ⇨ *GIMP Image Editor* F-Spot *Applications* ⇨ *Graphics* ⇨ *F-Spot Photo Manager*	GIMP is a pro-level image editor offering much of the functionality found in commercial applications like Adobe Photoshop. GIMP shouldn't be confused with F-Spot Photo Manager. This catalogs photos and allows simple image tweaking. F-Spot will automatically start when you attach a digital camera, and stores photos in the `Pictures` folder within your `/home` folder.

Type	Application	Details
Office suite	OpenOffice.org *Applications* ⇨ *Office* ⇨ *OpenOffice.org Presentation/ Spreadsheet/ Word Processor* OpenOffice.org Draw *Applications* ⇨ *Graphics* ⇨ *OpenOfice.org Drawing*	Office suite comprising a spreadsheet application (Calc), a word processor (Writer), a presentations package (Impress), and a vector graphics application (Draw). As with Evolution, the OpenOffice.org applications are closely modeled on Microsoft Office and offer a similar degree of usability. OpenOffice.org also includes a database application that isn't installed by default—just install the openoffice.org-base package (software installation is covered in Chapter 6).
Audio player	Rhythmbox *Applications* ⇨ *Sound & Video* ⇨ *Rhythmbox Music Player*	Audio player that's like Apple's iTunes, in that in addition to playing audio files, it also catalogs them for easy searching and the creation of playlists. Once the program starts, click Music ⇨ Import Folder and navigate to your store of MP3s. Note that Rhythmbox will offer to automatically install MP3 playback support the first time you attempt to play a file. Also note that files protected with Digital Rights Management (DRM), such as some songs purchased via iTunes, cannot normally be played on Ubuntu.
Video player	Totem *Applications* ⇨ *Sound & Video* ⇨ *Movie Player*	Capable movie playback application that comes complete with a browser plug-in that extends playback to Firefox. Totem will install support for various file formats when you first attempt to play them.
CD/DVD burning	Brasero *Applications* ⇨ *Sound & Video* ⇨ *Brasero Disc Burning*	CD/DVD burning program that's like Nero, used under Windows. The version provided with Ubuntu 8.10 can also create VCD/DVD movie discs.

Deskbar aims to be nothing more than a different way of accessing your computer. Want to open your Documents folder? Just click the Deskbar icon and type documents into the Deskbar text field that appears. Then select the Open Location option from the menu that appears (you can use the cursor keys to do this, rather than clicking the mouse; note that the most commonly-accessed entries will always be at the top of the list).

Want to visit a website? Type in the URL and select Open from the Deskbar menu. And, of course, if you wish to search for a file—or some text within a file—just type it into the Deskbar search field. The file will be listed within the results and you can select it to open it.

> **NOTE** To be able to search for files, or the contents of files, Tracker must be enabled, as described previously.

In fact, there's almost no limit to what Deskbar can search for and/or allow access to. It relies on a plug-in structure, meaning that new features can easily be added in. To see what plug-ins are installed, and activate/deactivate them, right-click the Deskbar icon and select Preferences from the menu that appears. Then, ensuring the Searches tab is selected, put a check alongside those you are interested in.

> **TIP** New applets, along with installation instructions, can be found at http://live.gnome.org/DeskbarApplet/Extending.

Keyboard shortcuts

Ubuntu makes use of a variety of keyboard shortcuts for quick access to built-in functions. Some of these shortcuts are similar to those found under Windows, while some are unique. See Table 3-2 for more information. Some of these shortcuts only work if desktop effects are enabled—see the *Graphics* section in Chapter 2.

Adding new users

It's easy to add new users to your Ubuntu setup. You might want to do this to give your children or spouse their own account.

As with Windows, you can create limited user accounts that stop the individual administering the system. Several entries are removed from the System ⇨ Administration menu, and if the user somehow bypasses this and runs some configuration software, their password simply won't be accepted as authorization.

Table 3-2. Useful keyboard shortcuts.

Key combination	Details
Alt+F4	Quit application
F1	Context-sensitive help
F10	Open a program's File menu; use left/right cursor keys to move between other menus
Alt+F1	Open main menu; use left/right cursor keys to move between menus
Alt+F2	Open "Run Application" dialog box, whereby applications can be started by typing their filenames
Alt+Tab	Switch between applications
Shift+Alt+up cursor	Switch between applications using a live preview of each window (like Mac OS's Exposé feature)
Ctrl+Alt+ left/right cursor	Switch between virtual desktops
Windows+E	Switch between virtual desktops by viewing a live preview of each desktop (double-click to select)
Windows+M	Invert colors on desktop (useful for partially-sighted people, or if using the computer at night)
Windows+N	Invert colors in top-most program window
Ctrl+Alt+ Backspace	Restart the graphical subsystem (X); should only be used in emergencies because the restart is instant and without confirmation—all data will be lost!
Alt+F9	Minimize window
Alt+F10	Maximize window
Alt+F5	Restore window after maximizing
Alt+F7	Allows you to move window using cursor keys; hit Enter when done
Alt+F8	Allows you resize window using cursor keys; hit Enter when done
PrintScreen	Take screenshot of whole desktop
Alt+PrintScreen	Take screenshot of currently active program window

CAUTION All users on the system can access each others' files within their /home folders on a read-only basis. Chapter 7 looks at setting-up encryption to protect sensitive data so only you can access it.

To add a new user, click System ⇨ Administration ⇨ Users and Groups. When the dialog box appears, click UNLOCK and enter your password when prompted. Then click the ADD USER button.

In the dialog that appears, at a minimum fill in the Username, Real Name, and password fields (as prompted, enter the password twice to confirm). In the Profile dropdown list, select Desktop User. If you wish the new user to be able to administer the system, select Administrator.

By clicking the User Privileges tab, you can assign the new user individual administrative powers. If the computer is a laptop, you may want to put a check alongside Connect to Wireless and Ethernet Networks, which will let the user join new wireless networks while out and about (this option is not available under Ubuntu 8.04). Additionally, if the user might attach new printers, put a check alongside Configure Printers (in 8.04 this is labeled Manage Printers).

Once done, click OK. The new user account will be created instantly. To switch into it, either logout of your account (System ⇨ Log Out; or System ⇨ Quit under Ubuntu 8.04), or click the Fast User Switcher at the top right of the screen—simply select the new user's name from the menu that appears (see Figure 3-3 for an example). This will temporarily allow you to login as the new user, although your user account will still be running in the background.

To switch back to your own account, either logout of the new account or select your account from the Fast User Switcher menu. Again, bear in mind the new user account will still be running in the background.

> **TIP** Ubuntu 8.10 includes a guest account feature that avoids the need to create an account for somebody who might want to use your computer for a few moments (for example, borrowing a laptop to check a favorite website). Just select the Guest Session entry on the Fast User Switcher menu. The Guest user can't administer the system and is locked out of the /home folder, so your personal data is safe from prying eyes.

Making programs start automatically

By clicking System ⇨ Preferences ⇨ Sessions, you can control what programs start when the desktop does, and also prune existing startup programs to optimize boot speeds.

To make a program start automatically, click the ADD button and fill in the Name and Command fields of the dialog box that appears (the Comment field is for information purposes only and can be left blank).

You will have to provide the command-line name of the program in the Command field. In most cases this is obvious—if you wanted Evolution to start, for example, you would simply type evolution. If in doubt,

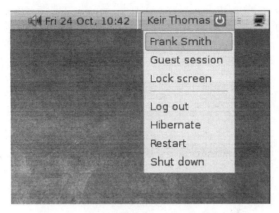

Figure 3-3. Switching user accounts.

open a Run Application dialog box by hitting Alt+F2. Then start typing the program's name in lower case. The name will autocomplete automatically after you've typed a few characters. Make a note, and hit Enter to run the program to ensure it is correct.

You can deactivate existing entries in the startup programs list by removing the check alongside them, but be aware that most entries are there for a good reason, and some control how vital background services operate. Only deactivate an entry if you're absolutely sure you can mange without it.

Dealing with crashed programs

If a program you've started crashes and won't quit, you can use System Monitor to terminate it. This program is found on the System ⇨ Administration menu. Ensure the Processes tab is selected, then locate the crashed program in the list. Right-click it and select Kill Process. Note that you won't be able to kill some programs because they are "owned" by the root user. This is discussed in more detail in Chapter 5, when we look at managing processes at the command-line.

Changing the time & date

To alter the time and/or date, right-click the time display at the top right of the screen and click Adjust Date & Time.

If using Ubuntu 8.10, make your changes in the dialog box that appears and click the SET SYSTEM TIME button. Type your password when prompted.

In Ubuntu 8.04, click the UNLOCK button in the dialog box that appears, type your password when prompted, then make your changes.

> **TIP** You can make Ubuntu automatically synchronize with Internet time servers, and therefore always have the correct time, by installing the ntp package. Software installation is explained in Chapter 6. Once ntp is installed, restart the computer.

Rebooting and shutting down

To shutdown or reboot the computer, click the Shut Down entry on the System menu (under Ubuntu 8.04, select the Quit entry). Then select the relevant option from the dialog box that appears.

> **TIP** You can also end your Ubuntu session by selecting the relevant entry the Fast User Switcher applet; see Figure 3-3 above.

Depending on your PC's hardware capabilities, you might also see options to suspend, and to hibernate. These are power saving modes, and the differences are as follows:

Suspend: This reduces power to all hardware devices with the exception of RAM. To "wake" the computer, you must hit a key, or press the computer's power button. The computer will come back to life within a second or two, and you can continue working in applications that were open prior to suspending.

Hibernate: This saves the contents of the RAM to hard disk and entirely powers-down the computer, as if it has been switched off. When the computer is next powered on, the contents of the RAM are loaded from disk, and you should find yourself back at the exact instant you chose to hibernate.

You should test either mode before relying on them. The hibernate mode in particular may or may not work correctly, depending on your hardware configuration. Always save data in any open applications before hibernating or suspending your computer.

> **TIP** To configure a laptop to automatically enter hibernate/ suspend mode when the lid is closed, click System ⇨ Preferences ⇨ Power Management, click the On AC Power/On Battery Power tabs, and choose the relevant option from the When Laptop Lid is Closed dropdown list.

CHAPTER FOUR

Users and the filesystem

The purpose of this chapter is to get you to speed with the Ubuntu filesystem. You'll learn about:

- How Ubuntu compares to Windows when it comes to files;
- Where things can be found in the Ubuntu filesystem;
- The basics of the users and permissions system that lies at the heart of Ubuntu;
- The Nautilus file manager;
- Useful filesystem tricks and tips;
- File compression.

How Ubuntu handles files

Some comparison between Windows and Ubuntu is inevitable when discussing the filesystem. Although fundamentally similar, as a variant of Linux, Ubuntu differs from Windows in the following ways.

Paths

There are no drive letters under Ubuntu. Instead, the root of the filesystem, known as `C:\` under Windows, is identified simply by a forward slash (/).

Additionally, whereas Windows uses a backslash (\) to indicate the root of the filesystem, and to separate folders in a path listing, Ubuntu uses a forward slash.

So, whereas a path like C:\Documents and Settings\Owner\My Documents is common under Windows, you will see something like /home/frank/Documents in Ubuntu. This difference can be jarring at first, but you'll be surprised at how quickly you get used to it.

Mounting

If there are no drive letters then how are other storage devices accessed, such as CD/DVD drives, or USB memory sticks?

The answer is that they're *mounted*—effectively, the filesystem of the storage device is magically plumbed through to a particular folder within the Ubuntu filesystem. Insert a CD/DVD, for example, and its contents will be visible when you browse to the /media/cdrom folder.

It's important to note that the files aren't literally copied to the folder. They're made available in a virtual way. You can manipulate the files and folders like any other files and folders, and although it might appear as if they're contained in that particular folder, they aren't.

Anything that might have already been in the folder used as the *mount point* will temporarily disappear. However, the contents are still there, and if the storage device is *unmounted*, the contents will reappear.

Mounting might sound complicated, but don't worry—it's nearly always done automatically, either at boot-up for devices permanently attached to your PC, or when you attach a removable storage device to the computer, such as a USB stick. You probably won't be aware of it taking place, in fact; all the user sees after inserting a USB memory stick is a new icon on the desktop that, when double-clicked, lets her browse the USB stick's files. Of course, if the user looks closely, she will see that she's actually browsing the folder that the USB memory stick has been mounted at.

File & folder names

File and folder names can contain spaces, as with Windows, but upper/lowercase letters are important in Linux. A folder can feasibly contain separate files called Report.doc, REPORT.doc, report.doc, RePORT.doc, and so on.

See Figure 4-1 for an example of this in action. The top half of the screenshot shows an attempt to rename a file to REPORT.doc in Windows, when a file called report.doc already exists in that folder. This isn't allowed because Windows is unable to tell the difference between

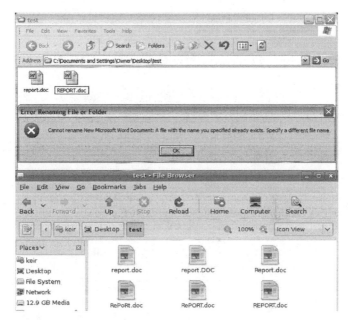

Figure 4-1. Windows top, Ubuntu bottom; upper/lower case matters in Ubuntu.

upper and lower-case letters—as far as it's concerned, report.doc is the same file as REPORT.doc. The bottom part of the screenshot shows a folder on an Ubuntu system containing several files that feature upper and lower-case variations of report.doc.

NOTE   This ability of an operating system to differentiate between upper and lower case letters is called *case sensitivity*.

Additionally, file and folder names under Ubuntu can contain practically any letter, number, or symbol, with the exception of the forward slash (/).

NOTE   Whereas Windows refers to *folders*, many Linux users refer to *directories*. Exactly the same thing is being discussed. The term *directory* is nearly always used at the command-line, although the term *folder* is preferred when using the Ubuntu desktop.

Important filesystem locations

Each user on the system is given their own folder within the /home folder in which to save personal data. For example, the user jane is

---

given the folder /home/jane. The /home folder is akin to C:\Documents and Settings under Windows.

> **TIP** Linux users often refer to their folder within /home as their "home folder", saying things like, "*I couldn't find the file but I remembered I'd saved it in my home folder.*"

Users aren't permitted to save their personal files outside of their /home folder. This is rigidly enforced using ownerships and file permissions, as I explain in the *Understanding Users* section below.

Outside of the /home folder, the Ubuntu filesystem is a little more complicated than Windows, and it isn't quite a case of program files being in one location, and system files in another.

A cursory rundown of the Ubuntu filesystem can be found in Table 4-1, although this is not essential knowledge and is provided largely for reference purposes.

Perhaps the most important locations for the majority of users are /home, as described above; /usr/bin, where practically all software is located; and /etc, where system configuration files are found.

> **NOTE** Like many versions of Linux, Ubuntu broadly follows the Filesystem Hierarchy Standard (FHS) to decide where things should go in the filesystem. For more details, including in-depth descriptions of each location, see www.pathname.com/fhs/.

Hidden files and folders

Windows lets users hide files and folders by setting a file attribute.

Linux takes a simpler approach. Any file or folder that has a period (.) at the beginning doesn't appear in file listings, unless the user specifically requests all files/folders be listed.

In other words, if you rename report.doc to .report.doc, it will instantly become invisible and will seem to disappear from the file browsing window (you might have to hit the Refresh button in the file browser window to update the listing before the file actually vanishes).

A user's personal configuration files are stored in his or her /home folder and are hidden in this way. To view them, and other hidden files, click View ⇨ Show Hidden Files in a file browsing window.

> **NOTE** Any file or folder that has a tilde (~) at the end of its filename (i.e. report.doc~) will be hidden in file listings provided by the Nautilus file manager, and on the desktop. They will be visible everywhere else, including at the command-line.

Table 4-1. Key locations in the Ubuntu filesystem.

Location	Details
/bin	Essential software, typically needed to get the system running
/boot	Files related to the boot menu/loader
/dev	Virtual files representing hardware devices
/etc	System (global) configuration files
/home	Users' personal folders
/lib	Support (library) files required by software
/media	Contains subfolders where storage devices can be mounted
/proc	Virtual folder containing files representing stats and settings
/root	Personal folder of the root user
/sbin	Essential software for system maintenance, usually used only by the root user
/tmp	Temporary files/folders
/usr	Essentially, subdirectories containing most software used on the system, including system libraries and documentation
/var	Data that is vital to the running of the system and that is constantly being updated

File extensions

Generally speaking, the trend in Linux is not to use file extensions for system files. Executable programs under Ubuntu don't have a file extension, such as .exe, as with Windows. Instead, the fact they are programs and not ordinary data files is indicated by the use of the executable file attribute. This is discussed in more depth in Chapter 5.

Configuration files sometimes have a .conf file extension, but often have no file extension at all. Many files that are plain text have no file extension, in fact; the use of the .txt file extension is rare in the world of Linux. Program documentation files in the /usr/share/doc folder, for example, are plain text and have no file extensions.

> **NOTE** It isn't quite true that files in the /usr/share/doc folder have no file extensions because some program documentation files are compressed, so have a .gz file extension, but this is a minor point.

However, when it comes to the personal files of users, such as documents or images, file extensions are as important as they are under Windows. Files with a .doc extension are recognized as Microsoft Word files, for example, and .jpg files are recognized as images.

Understanding users

When you installed Ubuntu, a personal user account was created for you. As part of this process, a folder named after your username was created in /home, as mentioned previously.

Root user

In fact, on most Linux systems *two* login accounts are created during installation—a standard user, and the *root user*. The root user is a special user account gifted with the ability to do anything, such as delete system files, or install software. Its username is always root.

Normally when Linux is used on a PC, a standard user logs into the root account whenever she has to administer the system, and then logs out when she's finished. However, she will spend most of her time logged into her ordinary user account, doing day-to-day stuff like browsing the web.

Ubuntu differs slightly from most Linuxes. Although the root account is there in the background, the user is discouraged from directly logging in as root. Instead, the user "borrows" root powers to administer the system when necessary. Usually, this is done by simply entering your login password when prompted. See Figure 4-2 for an example that appears when attempting to run Synaptic, a program that administers software. Synaptic lives on the System ⇨ Administration menu, and, in fact, if you run any program on this menu a password prompt dialog box will pop-up. You won't be able to get any further until the password is typed but, after this, the application will run with root powers.

Alternatively, some applications will start, but will have restricted functionality until the UNLOCK button is clicked, at which point the same password request will appear. With these applications, typing your password doesn't give the entire application root powers, but a component of it. This is more secure and, eventually, all of Ubuntu's administrative applications will work this way.

> NOTE When working at the command-line, any command needing administrative powers must be preceded by sudo (gksu should be used for GUI apps). I explain more about this in Chapter 5.

File permissions

Although the root user account has a back seat in Ubuntu, its influence is felt everywhere. Most operating system files are "owned" by the root user, and have permissions so that only root can edit them. In other words, only the root user—or *a user borrowing root powers*—can

Figure 4-2. Typing a password to borrow root powers and administer the system.

delete or modify vital files. In some cases, even viewing operating system files by ordinary users is prohibited.

This simple mechanism of protecting operating system files through root user ownership is how Linux enforces security and system protection. It's simple but highly effective, and has stood the test of time for many years.

NOTE The fact that Windows fails to make this distinction, and effectively merges the standard and administrator types of user account, is one reason it's so insecure. If a virus infects the system, it operates with administrator powers, so it can really cause trouble. Vista fixes this situation somewhat by pestering the user every time they do something even remotely dangerous to the system.

File permissions lie at the heart of understanding and working with the Linux filesystem, so let's take a look at them in more depth.

As mentioned previously, every file is owned by a particular user—even system files, which are owned by the root user.

The owner of a file can set three separate sets of permissions: firstly for himself, secondly for the group, and lastly for all others.

In setting file permissions for himself, the file's owner could mark a file as read-only, for example, to avoid accidentally changing it.

All users are members of a group, and each file is assigned to a particular group, in addition to being owned by a user. So, a separate set of file permissions can be granted for members of that group.

A third and final set of permissions can be configured for *others*, which is to say, users on the computer who aren't the file's owner, and who aren't in the group.

TIP When trying to comprehend how Linux handles files, it helps if you remember it's a clone of Unix, an operating system designed to have hundreds or even thousands of different users. One of the fun facts about Linux is that, although you might use it on your humble desktop computer, it really is capable of running on a mainframe computer without any adaptation.

You can view and edit file permissions for any file or folder by right-clicking it and selecting Properties from the menu. In the dialog box that appears, click the Permissions tab. You can only change permissions for a file or folder that you own.

Let's take a look at permissions in action. The user called frank creates a spreadsheet. He's a member of the accounts group, along with the user called jane, his colleague in the Accounts department. frank wants jane to be able to edit the spreadsheet, so he sets the group permissions for the file so that anybody in the accounts group can both read and write the spreadsheet. frank wants other people in the company to be able to *view* the spreadsheet, including users in other departments who aren't in the accounts group. Yet he doesn't want them to be able to *edit* it. So, he sets read-only permission for *others*.

In the case of operating system files, owned by the root user, permissions are normally set so that other users on the system can view (*read*) files, but not modify them (*write*). Important system folders are also protected in this way, so that new files can't be created there. The root user also owns the root of the filesystem (known as c:\ in Windows). This particular permission is "hard-wired", so that only the root user can create new files or folders there. Again, this is for security reasons.

NOTE Under Ubuntu, group file permissions are unimportant when it comes to files owned by root, because the root user is in a private group of its own, also called root.

We'll come back to file permissions in Chapter 5, which looks at the Linux command-line. It's at the command-line that file permissions become much more important, particularly when administering the system.

Nautilus: An overview

The file browsing program provided with Ubuntu is called Nautilus. It's a staple of the Gnome desktop environment and is extremely powerful, yet also user-friendly.

You can start Nautilus by clicking Places ⇨ Home Folder. This will let you view the contents of your personal folder within the /home folder.

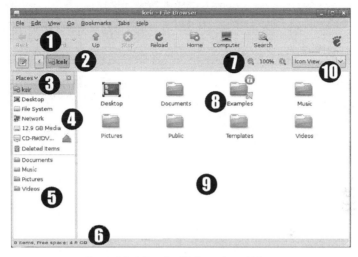

Figure 4-3. A Nautilus file browsing window.

Figure 4-3 is annotated to show what each component of the Nautilus program window does. The descriptions are as follows.

1. **Toolbar**: Here you can move backwards and forwards within your file browsing history, or click the UP button to move to the parent folder of the one you're currently browsing. The RELOAD button will refresh the file listing to show files that have recently been added or deleted, while the Home and Computer buttons provide shortcuts to those browsing locations.

   NOTE   The "Computer" location is equivalent to Windows' My Computer (*Computer* under Vista), and storage devices connected to the computer are listed.

   The SEARCH button starts Nautilus' file search function, described later in this chapter.

2. **Location bar**: The location bar displays the currently browsed folder, and works in one of two modes: *button*, and *text*.

   Button mode, activated by default, shows a button for each folder you browse to. For example, if browse to /home/keir/Pictures/Disneyland, there will be a button for Disneyland, a button for Pictures, and one for keir (the home

Figure 4-4. Nautilus' location bar modes side-by-side
(top: button mode; bottom: text mode).

folder doesn't get a button in order to save space). Clicking each button will take you straight to that particular folder.

Text mode is activated by clicking the button at the far left of the location bar, and is equivalent to the standard location bar found in most file browsers: the path is shown as text for informational purposes, but can also be edited to switch to a new location. See Figure 4-4 for both modes shown side-by-side.

3. **Side Pane**: The side pane shows information relevant to the files or folders being browsed. It can be closed by clicking the X button at the top right of the pane or, by clicking the dropdown list heading, can be switched into one of six modes, as follows:

    Places: This is the default mode and shows shortcuts to important filesystem locations, as well as providing one-click access to any storage devices attached to the computer. If the storage device can be ejected or needs to be unmounted before removal (i.e. a DVD-ROM drive, or a USB memory stick), an eject icon will appear alongside (Ubuntu 8.10 and above only).

    Information: This mode is similar to that found in some versions of Windows, and shows the name of the folder currently being browsed, along with the number of items it contains.

    Tree: This is the "traditional" view that appears in the left-hand pane of a file browsing window. The full filesystem is displayed. By clicking the chevron alongside each entry in the listing, you can "unfold" that particular folder to see what it contains. Selecting a folder will reveal its contents in the main browsing area.

History: This mode presents a list of locations you've visited in the current file browsing session, arranged in sequence. Clicking any entry will jump to that location.

Notes: Folders can have written notes invisibly attached to them, and the Notes mode lets you add, edit, or view this text. This can be useful in a very complex filesystem with lots of folders.

NOTE Both files and folders can have notes attached, although the side pane doesn't offer the ability to add them to files. To manually add a note to a file or folder, right-click it, click Properties in the menu, and select the Notes tab in the dialog box.

Emblems: Files and folders can have small icons affixed to them for informational purposes. Some of these have specific filesystem meanings, as discussed in the *Emblems* section below, but others are for the user's *aide mémoire* only. By selecting this side pane mode, a list of emblem icons are shown and these can be dragged and dropped onto any file or folder within the browsing window. To remove an emblem, just reapply the same emblem to the file/folder.

4. **Filesystem locations**: If the Places mode of the side bar is selected (it is by default), you'll find listed shortcuts to filesystem locations, or attached storage devices. This list is identical to the entries found on the Places main menu. In the example shown, the list reads as follows:

keir: This is a shortcut to the user's /home folder—in the case of the test PC used to create the screenshot, the user is called keir.

Desktop: As with Windows, files on the desktop are contained within a special folder in your personal /home folder called Desktop. Here you can switch to that folder instantly.

File System: This provides a link straight to the root of the main filesystem (/; equivalent to C:\ under Windows)

Network: Here you can browse for resources on other computers connected to the network, such as shared folders on Microsoft Windows computers. Equivalent to Network Neighborhood.

13.8GB Media: This is a shortcut to the Windows filesystem. The name of this icon is based on the size of the Windows partition; if the Windows partition was 500GB in size, for example, the label would read 500GB Media. In the case of the

PC used to take the screenshot, the Windows partition size was 13.8GB.

NOTE If you have more than two operating systems installed, all the operating system filesystems will be listed for access here. Additionally, or alternatively, if you have a hard disk partition used solely for storing files, that will also be listed here.

CD-RW/DVD-ROM: This icon allows quick access to the CD/DVD-ROM. The icon is usually named after the CD/DVD-ROM disc label, although in this example the drive is empty. Because the CD/DVD-ROM drive can be ejected, an eject icon appears alongside. The same icon appears alongside storage devices that need to be unmounted before removing, such as USB sticks.

Deleted Items: Here you can quickly see what's in the Waste-basket (aka Trash, and also known as the Deleted Items Folder).

5. **Bookmarks**: If the Places mode is selected in the side pane, here you'll find shortcuts to bookmarked filesystem locations. This list is effectively a mirror of the Bookmarks menu.

TIP New bookmarks can be created quickly by dragging the relevant folder to this area.

6. **Status bar**: If no files are selected, the status bar shows the number of files in the current folder, along with the free space on the disk. If files are selected, you'll see the number of files in the selection, along with their combined total size.

TIP To find out the total size of all the files in the folder, just hit Ctrl+A to select all files and check the status bar.

7. **Zoom controls**: Here you can set the zoom level of the current view, effectively making the icons bigger or smaller, but in the case of icon view (see *Icon/List View Selector* below) also showing fewer or more details—zooming in will show details such as file size and creation date.

8. **Emblems**: As mentioned previously, all files and folders can have small icons attached to them. These are called *emblems*, and it's important to note they're specific to Nautilus. They probably won't show up if you're browsing using a different file manager, or at the command-line.

The user can add her own emblems, although the system also reserves a handful for informational purposes. The two emblems attached to this icon were added by the system and show that the owner of the folder has set it as read-only for the current user (the padlock icon top right). Additionally, the arrow icon at the bottom right shows this folder is a *shortcut*—the Examples folder actually exists at the /usr/share/example-content location and not in this user's /home folder.

9. **File area**: Here is where the files/folders in the currently browsed folder are listed. Right-clicking in a blank space will bring-up a menu whereby new files and folders can be created.

10. **Icon/list view selector**: Here you can switch between three separate file listing view modes: *icon*, *list*, and *compact*.

   They are as follows:

   Icon: In this mode, files and folders are displayed as large icons.

   List: Files and folders are displayed in a list, alongside pertinent details, such as file size, and the date the file/folder was last modified. Folders have a chevron alongside them—clicking this "unfolds" a listing, showing the contents of the folder.

   Compact: This displays the files and folders in list format, but without any details and in several columns dependent on the width of the window (compact mode is only available in Ubuntu 8.10 and above).

Day-to-day file management

It should be obvious how to perform most everyday file management tasks because Nautilus is very similar to every other file manager you might have used. However, Nautilus offers a handful of unique features, and some tasks are a little more complicated than others. These are explained in this section. Additionally, see Table 4-2, which shows some useful keyboard shortcuts for use with Nautilus.

> **TIP** The Ubuntu desktop is "managed" by Nautilus, so the same techniques and keyboard shortcuts work there too, even if no Nautilus window is open.

Links and launchers

Ubuntu refers to a file shortcut as a *link*. As with Windows, links can point to files, folders or applications, and there are several ways of creating one. Perhaps the easiest is to use the middle mouse button (on most mice this is the scroll wheel) to click and drag the file to the location where you'd like to create the link. Then let go of the button and select Link Here from the menu that appears.

> **TIP** To create a link for an application or filesystem location that's on one of the main menus, just click and drag it from the menu using the left mouse button.

Alternatively, you can manually create a link by right-clicking a file or folder and selecting Make Link. This will create a link alongside the original file, which you can copy to a new location. However, this will only work if you have permissions to create a link in the location of the original file.

You can also create launchers.

A launcher is effectively a small file that, when double-clicked, starts a program. Launchers usually sit on the desktop or the panels. To create a launcher, right-click the desktop and select the relevant option from the menu. Fill in the Name and Command fields (Comment can be left blank). In the Command field, you'll need to type the program's command name as it's known to the system—see the *Making Programs Start Automatically at Boot* heading on page 46 to learn how to find this out.

Click the icon preview at the top left of the Create Launcher dialog box to choose an icon for the launcher. When done, click OK.

Bookmarks

It's possible to add Nautilus bookmarks for various locations in the filesystem. These are just like bookmarks you might use in your web browser—shortcuts that take you straight to where you want to be.

Bookmarks are viewable by clicking the Bookmarks menu and also in the lower half of the side pane if the Places sidebar is selected. To create a new bookmark of the current folder, either click Bookmarks ➪ Add Bookmark, or hit Ctrl+D. You can instantly create a new bookmark by dragging the relevant folder onto the bookmarks preview in the side pane. This will be listed on the Bookmarks menu too.

Tabbed browsing

New to Ubuntu 8.10 and later releases of Ubuntu is tabbed browsing in Nautilus. You may know of this feature from your web browser where it allows the simultaneous browsing of more than one location. To open a new tab, hit Ctrl+T.

Table 4-2. Nautilus keyboard shortcuts.

Keyboard combination	Action
Alt+left cursor	Move back in the file browsing history
Alt+right cursor	Move forward in the file browsing history
Alt+up cursor	Switch to the parent folder of the one you're currently in
Alt+Home	Switch to the user's /home folder
F5/Ctrl+R	Refresh the file listing, showing any changes made since the listing appeared
Ctrl+=/Ctrl++	Zoom in (show more details)
Ctrl+-	Zoom out (show fewer details)
Ctrl+0 (zero)	Zoom to default level
Ctrl+W	Quit file browsing window
Shift+Ctrl+W	Quit ALL file browsing windows
Ctrl+N	New browsing window
Ctrl+D	Add current location as bookmark
Ctrl+B	Edit bookmarks
Ctrl+T	New tab (Ubuntu 8.10 and above)
Ctrl+A	Select all files
F2	Rename selected file/folder
Ctrl+O	Open selected file/folder
Ctrl+I/Alt+Enter	Show properties of selected file/folder
Ctrl+Shift+N	Create new folder
Delete	Move selected item to Wastebasket (Trash)
Shift+Delete	Permanently delete selected item (bypass Wastebasket)
F9	Show/hide side pane
Ctrl+1	Switch to icon view
Ctrl+2	Switch to list view
Ctrl+3	Switch to compact view (Ubuntu 8.10 and above)
Ctrl+H	Show/hide hidden files
Ctrl+L (or hit forward slash)	Go to location (effectively, switch to text-based location bar rather than button mode; hit Esc to switch back)

Files can be dragged and dropped between tabs. To do so, drag the file or folder to the other tab, and Nautilus will switch to it automatically. Then release the mouse button. Alternatively, you can simply copy, cut and paste files in the usual way using the Edit menu.

Searching for files

Ubuntu offers two methods of searching for files: using the system-wide Tracker tool, as detailed in the *Desktop Search* section in Chapter 3, or using Nautilus' own more humble file search function. The two methods are independent, and you don't need to have Tracker enabled to use Nautilus' search functionality.

To use Nautilus' search function, click the SEARCH button on the toolbar, or hit Ctrl+F. Type part of the filename you're looking for and hit Enter. By clicking the plus sign icon in the list of results, you can further refine the search results by filtering by file type.

> **TIP** Nautilus also offers a quick and dirty search function for files in the current folder—just ensure the Nautilus window is the active window and simply start typing. A small search text field will appear at the bottom-right of the window, and files/folders will automatically be matched and selected as you type.

Special browsing locations

Nautilus isn't limited to your computer's filesystem. It is also able to browse FTP sites, and Windows shares (known as *SMB/Samba shares*). Click Go ⇨ Location, and type the address of the computer you wish to connect to, preceded by either smb://, for Windows shares, or ftp:// for an FTP site.

For example, to connect to a computer that's sharing files on the network called office_pc, I type smb://office_pc. To connect to an FTP site with the address ftp.example.com, I type ftp://ftp.example. com. Once the connection is made, you will be prompted for any username and/or password information.

Alternatively, for network shares you can click Go ⇨ Network and Nautilus will attempt to detect any shared resources nearby.

> **NOTE** Nautilus can also connect to SFTP sites too. Simply replace ftp:// with sftp://, followed by the address.

File Associations

Double-clicking certain files will cause them to open in appropriate applications. Double-clicking a movie file, for example, will open it in

Totem Movie Player. To open a file in an alternative application of your choice, right-click it and select Open with Other Application from the menu. Select the application from the list and click OPEN.

To change permanently the default application for all files of a certain type, right-click any file of that type and select Properties from the menu. Then, in the dialog box that appears, click the Open With tab, and select the radio button alongside the correct entry in the list. Click the ADD button to add an application to the list if it isn't shown. Click the CLOSE button when done.

File compression

For most everyday users, file compression is the process of taking many files and combining them into a single archive file that's shrunk so it takes up less disk space. This makes the files easier to transfer from computer to computer.

Most Windows users make heavy use the Zip file format, and this is fully supported in Ubuntu.

Double-clicking a compressed file of virtually any format will open it in the FileRoller program, which is a little like WinZip under Windows. To extract any file or folder within the archive, simply click and drag it to a new location.

To create a compressed file from a file or folder, just right-click it and select the Create Archive option. Select the compression type you'd like to use from the dropdown list alongside the filename.

> **TIP** There's one popular compression format missing from Ubuntu: rar. To add rar compressed file support to Ubuntu, install the rar and unrar software packages. Software installation is discussed in Chapter 6. Be aware that neither of these two software packages are Free Software, and that the rar software is a 40-day shareware demo—see the package description when installing to learn how to register.

Although Zip is popular on Windows, and there is no reason why it can't be used under Ubuntu, most Ubuntu and Linux users prefer a different type of compression: compressed tar files.

Tar has its roots in magnetic tape backup, hence the name: *T*ape *AR*chive.

A tar file is simply lots of files combined into a single large file. Tar files aren't compressed by default, which is to say, tar is not a compression

Table 4-3. Popular file archive types.

Archive file extension	Details
.tar	Tape ARchive; simple format in which files are combined into a larger file. Handled by the tar command at the command-line. Tar files aren't automatically compressed. The chief benefit of tar files is that they record permission and ownership details, making them ideal for backup.
.tar.gz	Tar archives that have been additionally compressed using the gzip software, usually at the point of creation.
.tar.bz2	Tar archives that have been additionally compressed using the bzip2 software, usually at the point of creation. Bzip2 compression leads to the smallest files of all, so is preferable.
.zip	As with Windows, zip files are compressed archives. Zip files haven't gained much traction in the Linux/Unix world because of legal concerns some years ago. This is no longer an issue, but other archive formats such as gzip and bzip2 are simply more established.

technology. However, tar files are nearly always compressed using add-in programs, the most popular of which are bzip2 and gzip. Tar files that are compressed usually have double file extensions showing the type of compression used: .tar.bz2 or .tar.gz.

NOTE   Sometimes individual files are compressed using bzip2 or gzip, without the need to create a tar file first. If this is the case, they simply have .gz or .bz2 extensions. This happens with the Ubuntu documentation contained in /usr/share/doc, for example.

Details of the most popular types of compressed file formats used under Ubuntu are listed in Table 4-3.

CHAPTER FIVE

Hands-on at the command-line

This chapter looks at what some consider the most fascinating and useful aspect of Linux: the command-line. The chapter explains:

- How to understand what the command prompt is telling you;
- How commands work (i.e. arguments and options);
- An overview of useful day-to-day commands;
- Tips and tricks to let you work efficiently;
- Using root powers at the command-line;
- Dealing with crashed or stalled programs;
- Understanding and manipulating file permissions;
- Advanced tricks (redirection, piping and brace expansion).

All about the shell

When we talk about the "command-line", we're talking about issuing typed commands directly to Linux. Most commands relate to manipulating files, while some administer the system. The command-line offers power and flexibility, at the expense of a slightly steep learning curve and—arguably—a lack of intuitiveness.

bashed about

The command-line utilized in Ubuntu is known as bash—the *B*ourne *A*gain *SH*ell. This is an evolved version of the Bourne sh program, one

---

of the oldest command-line programs for Unix. Most people agree that bash offers the best all-round mix of functionality and ease-of-use.

Command-line programs are sometimes known as *shells*, and the term comes from the fact that—like mollusks and crustaceans—the shell "wraps around" the delicate interior of the operating system, protecting it from accidental damage!

NOTE A graphical user interface is sometimes referred to as a shell because, by the above definition, it has the same function as a command-line prompt.

Other shell programs are sometimes used under Linux instead of bash. Perhaps the most popular are Korn Shell (ksh) and C Shell (csh). Both are geared towards programming and it's unlikely you'll ever come into contact with them. bash is the default in most popular Linux distros.

To DOS or not to DOS

You might be wondering if the Linux command-line is similar to Microsoft DOS. They're distant cousins rather than siblings. DOS was a clone of CP/M, that itself borrowed much from the Unix command-line. Some DOS knowledge will give you a head start, but you will have to unlearn as much as you learn!

Understanding the prompt

Let's get stuck-in straight away.

Starting a command-line session

There are two ways to start a command-line session: by running a desktop terminal program (sometimes known as a *terminal emulator*), or by switching to a *virtual console* (also known as a *virtual terminal*). In both cases you're accessing exactly the same command-line.

To switch to a virtual console, hit Ctrl+Alt+F2. The GUI will disappear and be replaced by a login prompt. Don't worry—your desktop is still there, and you can switch back to it by hitting Ctrl+Alt+F7. It's just that the virtual console needs to take over the screen.

NOTE There are *six* virtual consoles, and they're accessed by hitting Ctrl+Alt and F1, F2, F3, F4, F5 or F6. The console on F1 is used for debug and log output, so is best avoided.

Login by typing your username, and then the password. You won't be prevented from logging in because you're already logged in at the desktop—under Linux a user can login as many times as she wants.

As you might be realizing, a virtual console session is a little clunky. A more convenient way to access the command-line is to use a terminal program. This provides a command-line right there on the desktop.

Logout of the virtual console by typing exit, and switch back to your desktop (hit Ctrl+Alt+F7). Then open a terminal window by clicking Applications ⇨ Accessories ⇨ Terminal.

This time there's no need to login, because the terminal window runs as part of your desktop environment, and that's already logged-in.

> **NOTE** So why use a virtual console? Well, they're very useful when things go wrong. If the GUI crashes, you can switch to a virtual console to try and fix things. Even if there's no GUI subsystem, the virtual console will still be there. It's a permanent fixture of Linux.

Knowing who you are

When the terminal program appears, you'll see something like this:

- keir@keir-desktop:~$

This is the actual command-line prompt, often shorted to "prompt".

The first part of the prompt shows your username. In this example, taken from my test PC, the user is keir. After the @ sign is the name of the computer, commonly referred to as the *hostname*. This was set during installation of Ubuntu, on the same configuration screen where you chose your username.

The hostname is how the computer is known on the network. It isn't very important if your computer only connects to the Internet via a router or modem, but it's vital if Ubuntu is used in a server environment, or if you intend to remotely access it across the Internet.

As you can see, the computer in my test PC setup is called keir-desktop and so, reading the full prompt, we can see that the user named keir is logged in at (@) the computer named keir-desktop. In other words, the first part of the prompt is all about *who you are* and *where* you're logged in.

Knowing where you're browsing

After this is a colon. This separates the physical location part of the prompt from the rest, that tells us the location in the filesystem—which folder we're currently browsing. We see a ~ symbol (known as a *tilde*). This is shorthand that always indicates the user's /home folder. When you see a tilde, imagine the path to your home folder instead.

> **TIP** You can also use the tilde yourself when typing commands to save typing out the entire path to your /home folder.

So, reading from left to right, the prompt tells us that the user keir, logged in at the computer called keir-desktop, is currently browsing his /home folder—in this case, that's /home/keir.

The final component in the line is a dollar sign. This indicates that you're logged in as an ordinary user. If you ever log in directly as root (discussed in the *Working with Root Powers* section later in this chapter), the prompt changes to a pound sign (#; also called a hash sign).

Try switching to your Documents folder by typing the following (hit the Enter key when you've finished typing the line):

- cd Documents

> **NOTE** Remember: upper and lower case letters matter in Ubuntu! You must type Documents and *not* documents or DOCUMENTS!

The prompt will change to something like the following:

- keir@keir-desktop:~/Documents$

Once again, from left to right, the prompt says that the user keir on the computer called keir-desktop is browsing the Documents folder in his /home folder (i.e. /home/keir/Documents).

How commands work

One of the beautiful things about bash is that it is entirely logical. Nowhere is this better shown than with how commands work. Once you've figured out how one command works, learning the rest is easy.

Arguments

Some commands can be issued on their own. An example is ls, which will list files (the equivalent of dir, that you might have used under DOS/Windows). Try it now; open a terminal window if one isn't already open, and type ls. Here's what I see on my test PC:

- ls

```
Desktop    Documents    Examples    Music    Pictures    Public    ⏎
Templates    Videos
```

This is a listing of the files and folders in my /home folder.

While some commands are good to go on their own, most commands take *arguments*. In other words, they need to be told what file(s) or folder(s) to work with.

As mentioned, the cd (change directory) command is used to switch into another folder. It needs to be told what folder, so we supply this as an argument. The following will switch into the Documents folder:

- cd Documents

Some commands need more than one argument. Say that we wanted to copy the file report.doc from the Documents folder to the Desktop folder. The cp command is used to copy files and folders. We tell it the location and name of the file to be copied as the *first* argument, and specify the destination as the *second* argument:

- cp ~/Documents/report.doc ~/Desktop/

In this example, we've used the tilde symbol again as shortcut for the /home folder. From left to right, on my test system the command would translate as copy (cp) the file report.doc found at /home/keir/ Documents/ to the destination folder /home/keir/Desktop/.

Once a command is entered, all that's usually seen is the prompt again. There's no confirmation. bash doesn't say "OK" or "Command completed!". bash is the silent type. It'll only speak if it has to, usually to tell you of an error.

Command options

Most commands also have *command options*. These alter how the command works. Going back to the file listing command (ls), one problem is that it lists files without any additional information. What if we want to know who owns the files, or what permissions are set? For this we use the -l command option. Most command options are preceded by one or two hyphens, so that bash knows they're not arguments.

Here's the ls command used on its own, and then with the -l command option:

- ls

```
Desktop    Documents    Examples    Music    Pictures    Public    ↵
Templates  Videos
```

- ls -l

```
total 28
drwxr-xr-x 2 keir keir 4096 2008-10-24 10:07 Desktop
drwxr-xr-x 2 keir keir 4096 2008-10-24 10:07 Documents
lrwxrwxrwx 1 keir keir   26 2008-10-24 09:51 Examples ->    ↵
  /usr/share/example-content
        etc.
```

Another useful command option for `ls` is `-a`, which causes *all* files to be listed—even hidden ones.

Command options can be combined together. To do so, simply list them one after the other. To see all details about files, and also any hidden files, we would type `ls -la`.

`ls -la` is a very common command used by many Linux users daily.

Command options are usually letters, but sometimes words are used too. In fact, to view a quick list of options, you can use the `--help` command option (that's two hyphens, rather than one). For example, `ls --help`, or `cp --help`. This option works with virtually all commands.

Complex filenames

Filenames with spaces in them present problems because a space between items on a command-line is taken as an indication that command arguments or options follow.

For example, the `rm` command is used to delete files. If we wanted to delete a file called `third quarter report.doc`, and typed `rm third quarter report.doc`, we'd see the following series of error messages:

```
rm: cannot remove 'third': No such file or directory
rm: cannot remove 'quarter': No such file or directory
rm: cannot remove 'report.doc': No such file or directory
```

In other words, the `rm` command interprets each word in the filename as a separate argument—it thinks you want to delete a file called `third`, a file called `quarter`, and a file called `report.doc`.

The solution is simple—just wrap any file or folder name containing spaces in quotation marks:

- `rm "third quarter report.doc"`

This should be done for file/folder names that include symbols too.

> **TIP** Another method of dealing with spaces or symbols is to *escape* them. This involves typing a backslash (\) before each space or symbol. To delete the above file, you could type `rm third\ quarter\ report.doc`. Most times quotation marks work fine.

Relative and absolute paths

A *path* is simply the part of a file or folder listing describing where it is located in the filesystem—`/home/keir/Documents/report.doc`, for example. Paths can be expressed in two ways: *relative* and *absolute*.

Imagine that a user called Frank is using the command-line and is browsing his Pictures folder, whose location is /home/frank/Pictures.

NOTE Remember that the root of the filesystem, indicated by C:\ under Windows, is indicated in Linux by a single forward slash (/).

What if Frank wants to view photos from his vacation, and so wants to switch to the Disneyland folder, that is in the Pictures folder?

Frank's been paying close attention to this book, because he knows he can type the cd command, as mentioned above. But what should he type next?

He could type the full path to the folder, like this:

- cd /home/frank/Pictures/Disneyland

This works fine, but it's a lot of typing.

In the above command, Frank has specified the *absolute path* to the file—the full location, from the root of the filesystem up. Of course, it would make far more sense if Frank simply typed:

- cd Disneyland

After all, he's already browsing the Pictures folder.

Frank doesn't realize it, but here he has specified a *relative path*. Rather than provide the path from the bottom-up, he specified a filesystem location *relative* to where he's currently browsing.

NOTE The folder a user is currently browsing is sometimes referred to as the *working directory*.

Once Frank has switched into the Disneyland folder, he can switch back to the Pictures folder by typing the following:

- cd ..

The two periods are more command-line shorthand, this time indicating the parent folder of that being browsed.

With this in mind, what if Frank is browsing /home/frank/Pictures/Disneyland, and wants to switch to /home/frank/Music?

Frank could specify the absolute path (i.e. cd /home/frank/Music), but he can also use a relative path, like this:

- cd ../../Music

In this case, Frank has specified the parent of the folder he's browsing, and then the parent of that folder (i.e. the parent of the parent). At that point he's back in the /home/frank folder, so the final component of the command specifies the Music folder.

It's possible to navigate from any point in the filesystem to any other using a relative path. Of course, it's not always the most efficient way of working, and sometimes specifying an absolute path is quickest. It's down to the user to choose the best method each time.

Running programs

What happens behind the scenes when a command is typed?

First, bash checks to make sure the command isn't a *builtin*—a command that's part of bash itself.

If the command isn't a builtin, bash checks to see if the command is in one of the folders mentioned in the $PATH variable. This is a list of folders on the system that contain programs. You can view the $PATH on your system by typing echo $PATH at the command-line:

- echo $PATH

```
/usr/local/sbin:/usr/local/bin:/usr/sbin:/usr/bin:/sbin:/    ⤶
bin:/usr/games
```

bash searches through these in order, so looks first in /usr/local/sbin, and then in /usr/local/bin, and so on.

If the command isn't in any of the folders in the $PATH then bash gives up, and you'll see a "Command not found" error message.

> **NOTE** Actually, Ubuntu is a little cleverer than most Linuxes in this situation. Rather than immediately report a "not found" error, it will check to see if the command you typed is available for download and installation from the software repositories (see Chapter 6). If it is, you'll be told so, and even told how to install it!

What if you've manually downloaded a program to the folder you're browsing, and want to run it? Simply typing its filename won't work. bash will search the $PATH to look for the command.

Instead, a neat trick is used: the command is preceded by a dot and a slash. The following will run a program called browser that's been downloaded to the folder the user is currently in:

- ./browser

In the same way that two dots refer to the parent folder, a single dot refers to the current folder. Some people interpret the dot to mean "right here" and that's a handy way of thinking about it.

Another method of running the program is to type its absolute path. If browser is located in /home/keir, for example, it could be run by typing /home/keir/browser.

Useful everyday commands

Table 5-1 lists typical commands that are commonly used day-to-day in Ubuntu, along with popular command options. It's only a brief list, and emphasis is placed on file manipulation commands.

Software management commands are not included—those are listed separately in Chapter 6.

Table 5-1. Useful day-to-day commands.

Command	Description
ls	List files and folders.
	Typical example: ls -l
	-l : Long listing (show permissions, ownerships etc.)
	-a : Show all files, including hidden files
	-h : Show KB, MB etc., rather than bytes
cd	Change folder. Type cd .. to change to parent folder.
	Typical example: cd Documents
cp	Copy file or folder; first specify file (and path if necessary), then specify destination.
	Typical example: cp myfile.doc Desktop/
	-r : Copy folders too, including contents (otherwise folders will be ignored)
mv	Move file or folder; can also be used to rename files/folders if a new destination isn't specified. Note that, unlike cp, it is not necessary to specify the -r option in order to move folders.
	Typical example: (moving): mv myfile.doc Desktop/
	Typical example: (renaming): mv old.doc new.doc
rm	Delete file(s) or folder(s); multiple files/folders can be specified.
	Typical example: rm -rf myfolder
	-r : Delete folder; must be used if a folder is to be deleted
	-f : Force deletion; don't prompt user for confirmation when deleting (useful when deleting lots of folders, but must be used with care)

Command	Description
ln	Create a link to a file (similar to a shortcut under Windows); first specify the file (including path if necessary), and then the location where the link should be created. A different filename may be specified for the new link.

Typical example: `ln -s myfile.doc ~/Desktop/`

`-s` : Create symbolic link, rather than hard link. In nearly all situations, a symbolic link is preferable, making this practically a prerequisite command option

| less | Open specified plain text file in a viewer (use cursor keys to scroll; hit Q to quit). Useful for viewing configuration files. |

Typical example: `less myfile.txt`

| df | Show amount of free disk space on all attached filesystems. |

Typical example: `df -h`

`-h` : Show KB, MB, GB etc. rather than bytes

| free | Show amount of free memory. |

Typical example: `free -mt`

`-m` : Show output in megabytes, rather than kilobytes
`-g` : Show output in gigabytes
`-t` : Show totals column

| grep | Search through specified file for a word or phrase. First, specify the phrase, and then the file to be searched through. |

Typical example: `grep -i wireless myfile.txt`

`-i` : Ignore upper/lowercase when searching

| man | View the manual (man) page for specified command. A man page is built-in technical documentation—see Appendix B. |

Typical example: `man ls`

| nano | Simple text editor that's ideal for creating, editing or viewing files (particularly configuration files); hit Ctrl+J to re-justify current line should you create a line-break during editing. |

Typical example: `sudo nano /etc/fstab`

| umount | Unmount attached storage device. Not a typo! The command is *umount* and not *unmount*. Needs root powers. Specify the mount point. |

Typical example: `sudo umount /media/cdrom`

| locate | Find specified file; relies on a background database that is periodically and automatically updated. The database can be manually updated by typing the `sudo updatedb` command. |

Typical example: `locate filename.doc`

`-i` : Ignore upper/lowercase when searching

Working with root powers

It's generally discouraged under Ubuntu to log in as the root user. Therefore, administrative tasks are carried out by ordinary users who "borrow" the root user's powers.

Using sudo

At the command-line, you can force a command to run with root powers by preceding it with sudo (short for *super-user do*). For example, to install software using the dpkg command (discussed in Chapter 6), root powers are needed, so to use dpkg you would type something similar to the following:

- sudo dpkg -i package.deb

You'll be prompted for your password. Once this is entered, the command will complete.

If you run a graphical application from the command-line it's necessary to precede it with gksu instead of sudo. To most intents and purposes, gksu is identical to sudo. For example, to start the Synaptic software installation application, you would type gksu synaptic.

> **NOTE** If you're using Kubuntu, the kdesu command is used instead of gksu. It's identical in function to gksu. Under Xubuntu the gksu command is used, as with the main Ubuntu release.

Temporarily switching to root

Despite the desire of Ubuntu's developers to stop you logging in as root, it's possible to temporarily switch to the root user account. This is useful if you have a lot of administrative work to do, where typing sudo before each command can become annoying.

To switch to the root user temporarily, type the following:

- sudo su

After typing your password, you'll see that the command-prompt changes to a hash symbol, to indicate that you have root powers.

When you've finished your work and want to return to your ordinary user account, just type exit, or hit Ctrl+D.

Enabling root login

It's also possible to enable the root login account. This will make Ubuntu just like most other versions of Linux and Unix. The main benefit of this is that it will let you directly login as root at a virtual console—just type root as the username.

To enable the root login, type the following; this will assign the root user a password and thereby allow login:

- `sudo passwd root`

After typing your own password to authorize, you'll be prompted to create a new password for root, so do so.

Following this, in addition to logging in as root at a virtual console, you can switch to the root user in a terminal window by typing su -, and entering the new *root* password when prompted. Once the admin work is done, type exit to logout (or hit Ctrl+D).

> **NOTE** Enabling the root account login makes no difference to borrowing root powers using sudo or gksu—you'll still have to enter *your* login password. The only time you'll need to type the root password is when logging in as the root user.

It's even possible to login to a Gnome desktop session as root. Because of the real potential for a misclick disaster, this is considered insanely reckless and isn't permitted by default. However, for some major administrative operations, access to a root-enabled GUI can be useful.

To allow GUI login as root, click System ⇨ Administration ⇨ Login Window. Select the Security tab and put a check in the box marked Allow Local System Administrator Login. Then logout and back in.

Give it a try—type root as the username at the login screen.

> **TIP** When logged in as an ordinary user you can start a Nautilus file browsing window with root powers by opening a terminal window and typing gksu nautilus. However, close the window straight after you've finished with it, because that Nautilus window will be able to delete any file, anywhere on the system!

File permissions in depth

It's at the command-line where permissions become important.

The basics

In Chapter 4, I mentioned that every single file is owned by a particular user on the system, and that the owner can set permissions for who can *read* the file and also who can *write* to it (i.e. modify the file).

Firstly, he can set permissions for himself. He can deny himself complete access if he wants, but more usually he might choose to deny himself the ability to write to the file so he can't accidentally damage it—effectively, making it read only.

Additionally, each user is part of a group, and each file is assigned to a group. Further read/write permissions can be set to allow or deny read or write access by members of the group the file is assigned to.

A third set of read/write permissions can be set for *all other users* on the system, regardless of what group they're in.

Execute permission

In addition to reading and writing, another permission can be set for files: *execute*. This is what marks out a file as a program and not just another data file.

The idea of an execute permission can be confusing to Windows users. Under Windows, the .exe file extension is usually used to identify files that are programs. However, if the execute permission isn't set on a Linux file, the program is effectively just another data file, regardless of its file extension.

All this means that, if Frank was to manually download some software, he can set permissions for who can *run* the program. Again, three sets of permissions are available—for himself, the group the file is assigned to, and others. He could make it so that only he can run the program.

Folder permissions

Folders are a little different from files when it comes to permissions.

In order to understand how permissions apply to folders, it helps if you realize that, on a technical level, they're simply small files containing a listing of the files or subfolders the folder contains, along with some technical information. Commands that list or modify the contents of folders actually access or modify this small file.

Execute permission

When applied to a folder, the execute permission has nothing to do with running programs. Instead, the execute permission controls who can *access or modify* the small folder file.

In real-world terms, this means that if the execute permission for a folder isn't set, the contents of the folder are inaccessible.

Unless the execute permission is set for a folder, the user will be not be able to do any of the following:

- View a listing of files in the folder (with caveats—see later);
- Create, modify or delete files in the folder;
- Switch into the folder by double-clicking its icon using Nautilus, or using the cd command.

If a user attempts any of these actions, and the execute permission isn't set, she will see a "Permission Denied" error message.

As with files, execute permissions can be set for the folder owner, the group it's assigned to, and others.

Read/write permissions

Although the execute permission controls access to the folder, permissions for reading and writing can be set separately. However, *neither has any relevance unless the execute permission is also set.*

Read permission: By setting the read permission of a folder, it's possible to control who can view a listing of the files/folders there. If a user tries to view a file listing, and the read permission isn't set, he'll see a "Permission denied" error.

Write permission: By setting the write permission, it's possible to control who can create, delete or rename files/folders within a folder. If the folder's write permission isn't set, and a user attempts to create, delete or rename a file/folder, he'll see an error.

As with files, separate read and write permissions can be set for the owner of the folder, the group it's assigned to, and others.

Folder permissions in more depth

It isn't entirely true to say that users won't be able to view the listing of a folder unless the execute permission is set. If the read permission for a folder is set, but not the execute permission, users will be able to view a short file listing using the ls command but the long listing command option (i.e. ls -l myfolder) won't work. Why this happens is to do with the way Linux works on a technical level.

> **NOTE** In a Nautilus file-browsing window, if the read permission is set, but not the execute permission, the user will be able to access the folder but it will appear to be empty.

If all of this is giving you a migraine, don't worry. For most users, folder permissions boil down to the following day-to-day rules:

Read only: To limit a user to viewing a listing of files in a folder, ensure the read and execute permissions are set, but not the write permission;

Write permission: To let a user create or delete files in a folder, ensure the read, write and execute permissions are set (note: it's possible for a folder to be set to "write-only" if the read permission isn't also set—users will be able to save files there, but not view a file listing);

Deny access: To deny complete access to a folder for a user, unset all permissions—read, write, and execute.

Any other combination of folder permissions can lead to confusion.

What permissions look like

Within a command-line file listing, permissions are indicated by r, for read, w, for write, and x, for execute. For all files and folders, the permissions are listed in a line: owner first, followed by group, and then others. See Figure 5-1 for an annotated example.

Permissions, ownerships and group assignments can be viewed by using the -l command option with the ls command. Give it a try by listing the permissions of files and folders in your /home folder:

- ls -l ~

Here's what I see on my test system:

```
total 28
drwxr-xr-x 2 keir keir 4096 2008-10-24 10:07 Desktop
drwxr-xr-x 2 keir keir 4096 2008-10-24 10:07 Documents
lrwxrwxrwx 1 keir keir   26 2008-10-24 09:51 Examples ->    ↵
/usr/share/example-content
drwxr-xr-x 2 keir keir 4096 2008-10-24 10:07 Music
drwxr-xr-x 2 keir keir 4096 2008-10-24 10:07 Pictures
drwxr-xr-x 2 keir keir 4096 2008-10-24 10:07 Public
drwxr-xr-x 2 keir keir 4096 2008-10-24 10:07 Templates
drwxr-xr-x 2 keir keir 4096 2008-10-24 10:07 Videos
```

Let's take a closer look at the first in the list—the Desktop folder. The permissions, ownership and group assignment are listed at the beginning of the line and read as follows:

```
drwxr-xr-x 2 keir keir
```

The d at the beginning simply indicates this is a *directory*—another word for a folder. If a hyphen appears there instead then we're dealing

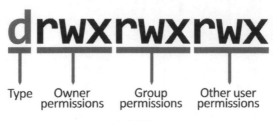

Type   Owner   Group   Other user
       permissions   permissions   permissions

Figure 5-1. File/folder permissions.

with a file. There are a handful of other letters that can appear here, but the main one you'll encounter is l, which indicates a link.

Following this are the three sets of permissions, listed one after the other: rwxr-xr-x. After that is a link number, which isn't relevant to this discussion and can be ignored. Then the owner's username is listed (in this case, keir), and then the group the file is assigned to (the group is also called keir).

> **NOTE** Under Ubuntu each user is assigned to their own personal group, that is named after their username. This policy effectively means that group permissions are irrelevant for personal files unless you were specifically to add another user to your personal group. However, it's still important you understand the concept of groups and how it applies to file/folder permissions.

Here are the permissions separated out into sets of three relating to owner, group and others:

```
Owner: rwx
Group: r-x
Others: r-x
```

The owner has read (r), write (w), and execute (x) permissions. In other words, he can do anything—he has full permissions. He can view a file listing of the Desktop folder, and write new files there. He can switch to the folder by typing cd Desktop, or by browsing to it with Nautilus.

Members of the group keir have read and execute permissions, so they can view a file listing of the folder, and also switch into it. However, they can't write any files there, or delete them, because there's a hyphen where the w would normally appear. Quite simply, a hyphen in place of a permission means "no permission".

Finally, other users on the system also have read and execute permissions, but not write permissions—just like with the group permissions.

Let's take a look at another example of permissions, this time from a word processing document called report.doc:

```
-rw-r--r-- 1 keir keir 3024 2008-10-28 18:21 report.doc
```

Once again, we see that the file belongs to the user named keir, and is assigned to the group named keir.

This time the permission component of the listing starts with a hyphen, because this is a file and not a folder or link. Following this are the three groups of permissions that again can be split-out as follows:

```
Owner: rw-
Group: r--
Others: r--
```

The first permission grouping refers to the owner, and he can read and write to the file, but not execute it. That makes sense because this is a document file and not a program; nobody would want to execute it.

Next, the group permissions say that any member of the group called keir can read the file, but not write changes to it (there's a hyphen where the w would be), or execute it.

Finally, others on the system can also read the file, but not write changes to it or execute it.

In other words, for everybody but the user named keir, the file is read-only.

Changing ownerships and permissions

Files or folders can have their ownership and group reassigned, but root powers are usually needed to do so.

> **NOTE** A user can reassign the file's group without root powers, but only if they're a member of that group.

The owner of a file or folder can change its permissions so that read, write and execute permissions are either added or removed. Root powers aren't needed for this.

Changing file ownership and group assignment

The chown (change owner) command is used to change a file or folder's ownership. It must be preceded by sudo, because changing a file or folder's ownership requires root powers.

The following will switch ownership of the file report.doc to the user frank:

- `sudo chown frank report.doc`

The chgrp (change group) command is used to reassign a file or folder's group. The following assigns the file report.doc to the accounts group:

- `sudo chgrp accounts report.doc`

However, you can reassign the owner and group in one fell swoop by using chown and separating the new owner and group assignment with a colon. The following will change the ownership of report.doc to frank, and change the group assignment to accounts:

- `sudo chown frank:accounts report.doc`

Changing file permissions

The chmod (change mode) command is used to alter permissions.

There are various ways of using the chmod command, but the easiest is to first specify who you want to alter the permission for (owner, group, or others) and then specify the permission changes (i.e. whether to add/remove read, write or execute permissions). Following this, the file or folder name should be specified.

Whom permissions should be changed for is indicated by u, g or o, standing for user (i.e. owner), group or others. The letter a can be used to indicate all three.

The permissions are indicated by r, w or x for read, write or execute, and whether the permission should be added or removed is indicated by the use of a plus or minus symbol (+/-).

Let's go back to the file report.doc that, you may recall, had the following permissions and user/group ownerships:

`rw-r--r-- keir keir`

The owner can read/write to the file, but everybody else (group and others) can only read the file.

If we wanted to allow members of the group to be able to write to the file, we could type the following:

- `chmod g+w report.doc`

In other words, this adds (+) write permissions (w) for report.doc's group (g).

If we were feeling generous and wanted to let other users to write to it too, we could type the following:

- `chmod o+w report.doc`

This adds (+) write (w) permissions for others (o).

On the other hand, if we wanted strict secrecy so that only the file's owner could read or write to the file, and nobody else, we could type the following:

- chmod go-rw report.doc

This removes (-) read and write permissions (rw) from report.doc for the group and others (go). If anybody apart from the owner should subsequently try to view or modify report.doc, they'll get a "Permission denied" error.

> **TIP** A quick way of removing *all* permissions for a type of user is to use the equals sign (=). For example, to remove all permissions for the group, you'd type chmod g= report.doc. This is the equivalent of typing chmod g-rwx report.doc.

Changing folder permissions

Folders are handled in the same way, although to allow/deny access to the folder, the execute (x) permission is set/unset.

The following will stop everybody apart from the folder's owner reading a file listing of the Documents folder, reading/writing files, and switching into the folder:

- chmod go-rwx Documents

In other words, this makes the folder entirely private.

> **NOTE** Don't forget that the root user can access all files and folders, no matter what their ownership or permission. It's worth mentioning with respect to privacy that the Ubuntu boot menu's Recovery option allows anybody using the computer to login as root, with no password required. Because of this, true privacy of files is only guaranteed via encryption, as explained in Chapter 7.

Subfolders within a folder inherit the execute permissions of the parent folder. In other words, if it's not possible to access the Music folder because the execute permission isn't set, you won't be able to access a folder within it *even if permissions are set correctly for that subfolder.*

Special permissions

In addition to read, write and execute, there are three other types of permission you might encounter: Set user ID (SUID, or SETUID); Set Group ID (SETGID); and the "sticky bit".

These might be described as specialist permissions with specific system administration uses, and it's unlikely you'll need to make use of them day-to-day. They operate as follows:

Set User ID: In its most typical use, the SUID permission allows a program to run as if the program's owner was running it (in other words, it runs with the permissions of the file owner, rather than the user who's running it). It's most commonly used to allow ordinary users to run programs with root powers, without the need to use sudo or switch to root user first. Such a program would be owned by root, will be set as executable, and have the SUID permission set. The s permission must be specified with chmod to set SUID (i.e. sudo chmod u+s *programname*). The SUID permission shows-up in long file listings as an s in place of the usual x that marks an executable file (i.e. -rwsr-xr-x).

> **NOTE** Under Ubuntu the SUID permission has no relevance when applied to folders, and is ignored if set.

Set Group ID: As with SUID, the Set Group ID permission causes a program to run with the permissions of its group. However, SETGID is mostly used with folders, where it forces all files or subfolders created within the folder to inherit the group permission of the folder, rather than the user who created it. As above, the s permission is specified (i.e. chmod g+s *myfolder*), and the permission shows up as s in file listings.

Sticky bit: When set on a folder, the sticky bit means that only the owner of a file or subfolder within that folder can delete it (although the owner of the folder itself will be able to delete the file, as can root). The sticky bit is useful for folders where files are shared, but the administrator doesn't want users to be able to delete any other user's files. The sticky bit is indicated in file listings by a t at the end of the permission listing (i.e. drwxrwxrwt), and is set by typing chmod +t *foldername*. When applied to a file within Ubuntu, the sticky bit is meaningless and is ignored.

> **NOTE** Should you see a capital S or capital T within file listings, instead of lower case letters, the execute permission hasn't been set for the relevant file or folder. Although SUID and sticky bits normally rely upon the file/folder being executable, they don't automatically set it.

Table 5-2. bash keyboard shortcuts.

Key combination	Details
Up/down cursor key	Scroll through command history
Ctrl+left/right cursor key	Move cursor from word to word
Tab	Autocomplete command or filename/path
Ctrl+A	Move to beginning of line
Ctrl+E	Move to end of line
Ctrl+W/Alt+Backspace	Delete word behind cursor
Alt+D	Delete word in front of cursor
Ctrl+U	Delete to beginning of line
Ctrl+K	Delete to end of line
Ctrl+Y	Restore text you've deleted
Ctrl+L	Clear screen (actually, this simply moves the prompt to the top of the screen; existing commands are still visible if the terminal window is scrolled)
Ctrl+C	Quit current program
Ctrl+Z	Switch current program to background (see *Job Management* section)
Ctrl+R	Search through command history
Ctrl+D	Logout (technically, terminate input)
Ctrl+T	Swap the two characters behind cursor

bash productivity tricks

bash is the result of many years of computing research, and has evolved into an ultra-efficient piece of software.

The key to being a bash master is to make use of keyboard shortcuts, and the *command history*—essentially, a list of commands you've already issued. Additionally, bash has built-in *job management*. This means you can start a program, switch it to the background, and get on with something else while it completes.

Keyboard shortcuts

Table 5-2 lists bash keyboard shortcuts with reference to a modern PC keyboard. Some of the shortcuts refer to the command history, as explained in the next section.

Perhaps the most useful keyboard shortcut is to hit the Tab key. This autocompletes commands and/or filenames. Most commands are short enough to be typed manually, but some filenames and paths can be long and therefore irritating to type.

Say you wanted to delete (rm) the file verylongfilename.doc. You could type rm very and hit Tab to autocomplete the filename.

Give Tab autocomplete a try. It's more intuitive than it might sound.

> **TIP**   Tab autocomplete also works when installing programs using the apt-get or dpkg commands, as described in Chapter 7. It will autocomplete package names based on what's in the repositories.

Command history

Every time you type a command at the prompt, it's remembered. A rolling list of 500 commands are recorded, in fact, and you can see a list of them by typing history at the command prompt.

> **TIP**   If you only want to look at the last 10 commands, you could type history 10. For the last 20, type history 20, and so on.

Commands are remembered so you can reuse them. You can cycle through the history list, from the most-recently-typed command up, using the up/down cursor keys (Ctrl+P and Ctrl+N do the same thing).

Alternatively, you can reuse any command in the history list by typing its number (as shown by the history command), preceded by an exclamation mark. If you want a view a file listing of the Documents folder, and ls Documents is command #480 in the list, you could type !480.

Here's another great trick: say you've just typed a long file copy (cp) command, and want to use it again. Typing !cp will find the last line in your history list that begins with cp and reuse it.

There are other neat history shortcuts too. Typing two bangs (!!) will cause the last command you typed to be reused. Typing !? and then part of a recently-typed command will cause bash to autocomplete using the nearest match it can find in the history. For example, typing !?upd on my system caused bash to reuse the sudo updatedb command, that was #471 in my computer's history list.

Hitting Ctrl+R lets you interactively search the history—just start typing the first part of the command, and bash will fill in the rest, guessed from your history. If bash autocompletes with an entry from your history that's incorrect, hit Ctrl+R again to step further back through your history to see another match until you find the one you're looking for.

There's a lot more to the command history function provided by bash. You're advised to read the history man page by typing man history.

> **TIP** If ever you want to clear your history, just type history -c. Incidentally, the history data is kept in a simple text file called .bash_history in your /home folder.

Job management

Thanks to the astonishing power of modern computers, very few commands take a long time to complete.

> **NOTE** Bear in mind that modern computers are like gods compared to the room-sized computers that Unix was first developed on in the 1970s and 80s. Because of this, some of bash's features can seem a little redundant in our modern day and age, but it's surprising how often they come in useful.

However, even though most commands complete in the blink of an eye, it's often useful to be able to run a particular command in the background, in order to get on with something else.

For example, the updatedb command updates the database of files used by the locate file search command. You can run it from the command-line by typing sudo updatedb. If you do so, the prompt will be tied up for up to a few minutes, during which you won't be able to work unless you open a new terminal window.

To avoid this, you can set the command to run in the background after starting by adding an ampersand (&) character to the end:

- sudo updatedb &

You'll be told the job number (in square brackets), and can switch to the new job by typing fg.

Alternatively, you can start the command as usual and hit Ctrl+Z. This will then put the command to the background, returning control of the prompt to you. Again, you can switch back by typing fg.

An example of how this might be useful might be if you're editing a file using a text editor. By hitting Ctrl+Z, you can temporarily abandon the text editor to do something else, and type fg to switch back to it when you need to.

Many jobs can be started as background tasks, and you can list them using the jobs command. You can switch to individual jobs by typing a percentage symbol and the job number—for example %2 will switch to job #2 in the list.

Managing processes

One of the commonest command-line tasks is clearing-up programs that have crashed, something known as *managing processes*.

On a technical level, Linux refers to currently running programs as *processes*.

> **NOTE** Some programs start more than one process, so perhaps a better definition of a process is that it is all or part of a program, and not necessarily an entire program.

You can see a constantly updating list of processes by typing the top command in a terminal window (hitting Q will quit when you're done).

As with files and folders, all processes are "owned" by a user. Only the individual who owns a process can terminate it, although the root user has the power to terminate any process.

The majority of processes listed in top are started at boot-up. These provide essential background services, such as the GUI. Such processes are usually owned by the root user. This protects them from interference by ordinary users.

All processes are numbered. The number is known as the *Process ID*, or *PID*, and this is listed on the left of each entry in the top program list. To force a process to quit—known as *killing* the process—hit K and type the PID. You'll be asked what signal you wish to send. Hitting Enter selects the default (15). This is fine in most cases.

You can also use the ps command to list processes at the command-line, and find-out process IDs. Normally the a, u and x command options are used with ps, and cause the command to return a full list of all processes complete with their names.

Additionally, the output is usually "piped" into the grep command to search for the program you're interested in. I discuss piping in the *Advanced Bash Techniques* section later, but for now it's enough to know that piping "sends" the output of one command into another.

Let's look at an example. Although Firefox very rarely crashes, let's say that you've visited a website that's caused it to lock-up. All attempts to quit the program in the usual way no longer work.

The following command will search the list of running processes and return the PID of Firefox:

- `ps aux|grep firefox`

The PID is the first number listed on each line in the results, and on my test PC the PID for Firefox was 15994. Knowing this, I was able to use the kill command, as follows:

- kill 15994

This caused Firefox to instantly quit. Bear in mind that, if you kill a program in which you are editing data, you won't be prompted to save it first. The kill command shows no mercy!

Another method of killing a program is to use the killall command. This lets you specify a command name, rather than the PID. So, to terminate Firefox, you could type the following:

- killall firefox

The downside of killall is that you need to know the program's command name. ps aux can be used to discover this. killall also, as its name suggests, kills all examples of the process with the specified name.

If you need to kill a root-owned process, simply precede kill or killall with sudo. Be very careful killing root-owned processes, however, because they tend to be related to the running of background services. Additionally, background service processes frequently spawn their own set of processes, and killing the *parent* process will in most cases also kill its *child* processes—often with disastrous results.

Working with compressed files

As mentioned on page 65, a variety of file compression and archive types might be encountered by the typical Ubuntu user. However, the two main types are zip files, as used in the world of Windows, and compressed tar archives.

Zip files

The following will create a new zip file called report.zip, and add report.doc to it:

- zip report.zip report.doc

To zip a folder full of files, add the -r command option. The following will create reports.zip, containing the contents of the reports folder:

- zip -r reports.zip reports

> NOTE If any files or folders have spaces or unusual characters in them, enclose them in quotation marks.

To unzip files, the unzip command is used. The following will extract the files from archive.zip:

- unzip archive.zip

To list files in an archive prior to unzipping, use the -l command option:

- unzip -l archive.zip

You can subsequently unzip a single file from the archive by specifying its filename (and path, if it's contained within a subfolder within the zip!) after specifying the archive name. The following will extract only report.doc from archive.zip:

- unzip archive.zip report.doc

tar archives

The tar command is both powerful and multi-faceted. It was originally designed for backup purposes, but works equally well for individual file/folder archiving.

The elementary creation and extraction of tar archives is described in this section. The curious reader is advised to search online for more complete guides, of which there are a great many.

Creating a tar archive

The following will create a simple tar archive called archive.tar, containing the contents of the reports folder:

> **NOTE** Remember that tar archives are not automatically compressed. They are simply container files. A tar file's size reflects almost exactly the combined size of the files it contains:

- tar cf archive.tar reports

The -c command option tells tar to create an archive, and the -f command option tells the tar command that the filename immediately follows. The -f option should always be added at the end of the range of command-options, immediately before the archive's filename.

> **NOTE** You might be wondering why the hyphen isn't used before command options with the tar command. The answer is that it's optional and so most people leave it out. A minority of commands make the hyphen optional, but most require it.

To additionally compress the archive, the -j or -z options can be added in for bzip2 or gzip compression, respectively. Bzip2 compression is considered most efficient and is arguably most common. Note that the user should manually add the bz2 file extension to the archive name. It isn't added automatically. The standard protocol with compressed tar files is to add two file extensions—one to indicate the file is a tar file, and one to indicate the type of compression.

The following will create a bzip2 tar archive of the reports folder:

- `tar cjvf archive.tar.bz2 reports`

The -v command option has also been added above. This provides *verbose* feedback, explaining what tar is doing. Without it, tar provides no feedback at all unless something goes wrong.

Extracting from a tar archive

The process of extracting files from an archive is largely the same as creating an archive. Instead of the -c (create) command option, the -x (extract) command option is used. The same -j or -z options should be added in the case of gzip or bzip2 compression, and the -f command option should be added at the end of the range of command options to specify that the filename follows.

The following will extract the contents of archive.tar.bz2:

- `tar xjvf archive.tar.bz2`

Again, the -v option has been added so that the user is provided with verbose feedback.

The following will extract the contents of archive.tar.gz:

- `tar xzvf archive.tar.gz`

NOTE If you're concerned that these chains of command options will be hard to learn then don't worry. They'll slip into your memory surprisingly easily after you've used them a few times.

To list files in an archive, use the -t option:

- `tar tjf archive.tar.bz2`

To extract a single file, specify it after the archive name. The following will extract report.doc from the archive.tar.bz2 archive:

- `tar xjvf archive.tar.bz2 report.doc`

If the file you want to extract is contained within a subfolder within the tar file, you'll need to specify that in the filename component.

Enclose any filenames/paths in quotation marks in the event of spaces or unusual characters.

TIP If you're interested in using tar archives for backup purposes, take a look at the Simple Backup Suite software. This automates the procedure via a GUI. Just install the sbackup package. Software installation is covered in Chapter 6.

Advanced bash techniques

Although they might be classed as advanced command-line skills, *redirection, piping* and *brace expansion* are not hard to understand. However, the fact they will only find use by more advanced users puts them outside the scope of this book, and they're explained here in a concise manner.

Redirection

Sometimes it's useful to send the output of a command into a file, rather than displaying it on screen. This is the principle of output redirection.

Let's say you wanted to make a permanent record of a file listing. To do this using redirection, type the following:

- `ls > listing.txt`

The right angle symbol (>) tells bash to redirect output of the ls command into the file listing.txt, rather than send it to the screen. Think of the angle-bracket as a funnel—the output of the ls command is "poured" into the listing.txt file.

If listing.txt doesn't exist, it will be created. If a file of that name already exists, its contents will be overwritten. Using two angle brackets (>>) instead of one will cause the output to be added to the bottom of an existing file.

You can view your new file in a text editor, or by using the less text viewer:

- `less listing.txt`

To redirect the contents of a file into a particular command, the reverse angle bracket is used (<). Not all commands are designed to take redirected input, of course, but the sort command is one of them. It can be used to alphabetically sort a list. If we had a file called shoppinglist.txt, that contained a list of products we wanted to buy from the store, and we wanted to sort the list alphabetically, we could redirect the contents of the file into the command, like so:

- `sort < shoppinglist.txt`

Piping

Piping is similar to redirection except that it's used to pass the output of one command to another—rather like connecting a pipe between the two commands, in fact!

The pipe symbol (|) is used for this purpose. On most keyboards this symbol can be found by hitting Shift and backslash.

Taking the previous example, if we wanted to pipe the output of the ls command into sort, to alphabeticize it, we would type the following:

- ls|sort

A common use of piping is to pass the output of a command to the grep command, which searches for a word or phrase. For example, if you have a huge file listing containing hundreds of files/folders, and want to find if report.doc is amongst them, you could type the following:

- ls|grep report.doc

Incidentally, if you see no output, the search phrase wasn't found.

Brace expansion

Brace expansion is a labor-saving trick. It's best explained by example.

Let's say you've come back from a European tour with a digital camera full of photos, and want to create four folders on your PC, named photos_germany, photos_france, photos_england, and photos_spain. You could create each manually using the mkdir command, but brace expansion lets you to create all four in one fell swoop, as follows:

- mkdir photos_{germany,france,england,spain}

If we view a file listing, we'll find we have four new folders:

- ls

photos_england photos_france photos_germany photos_spain

In other words, anything within the braces ({}) is individually added to photos_ and a new folder is created using that name. Each item within the braces should be separated by a comma.

If you subsequently wanted to delete the photos_spain and photos_france folders, rather than type two separate rm commands, you could use brace expansion again:

- rm -r photos_{france,spain}

Brace expansion works with all commands, not just mkdir and rm, and is packed with features. For example, rather than specifying individual expansions separated by commas, a range of letters or numbers can be specified. If you wanted to create 10 folders named photos (i.e. photos1, photos2, etc.), the following will do the trick:

- `mkdir photos{1..10}`

Letters can be specified instead of letters. The following will create photosA, photosB etc., all the way to Z:

- `mkdir photos{A..Z}`

Wildcards

Worth mentioning alongside brace expansion is the concept of *wildcards*. The term is taken from Poker, where a card that's "wild" can represent any card. This might help you understand wildcards at the command-line: they're symbols that specify any character(s).

The most commonly-used wildcard is the asterisk (*), used to indicate any combination (or number) of characters.

If you wanted to delete all files in a folder, you could type the following:

- `rm *`

In this example, the asterisk wildcard represents any filename that contains any number of characters. That's all of them!

To return to the vacation folder example used above, the photos_spain, photos_germany etc. folders could be deleted like this:

- `rm -r photos_*`

This will delete any file whose name begins with photos_, but has *any number of characters* following (should there be a folder called photos_, with nothing after it, that too will be deleted).

A question mark (?) can be used to indicate any *single* character. The following will delete photos1, photosA, photos!, and so on:

- `rm -r photos?`

The following will delete photos1, photos3 and photos4, but leave in place any other folder named photos and followed by any character:

- `rm -r photos[134]`

In other words, each character within the square brackets is individually substituted within the filename, in a similar way to brace expansion. However, wildcards are designed to match patterns of characters in *existing files* (or data), so won't work when creating files.

CHAPTER SIX

Software management

This chapter looks at how to install and remove software, and manage the software subsystem. You will explore the package management system that lies at the heart of Ubuntu. Topics covered include:

- An explanation of the package management subsystems;
- Installing and removing software using Synaptic;
- Manually installing a software package;
- Installing and removing software at the command-line;
- Adding new software repositories;
- Compiling a program from source code.

All about package management

Like many versions of Linux, Ubuntu relies on a system called *package management* for all its software installation and removal needs.

What's in a package?

Nearly all Ubuntu programs are distributed as *software package* files.

Package files are similar to installation setup.exe files under Windows, in that they're single archives containing a program's components. When the program is installed, the components are unpacked onto the hard disk, and the system configured so the software will work.

However, a key difference with Ubuntu is that packages only contain the program itself. Typical setup.exe files for Windows include the program and also various system files that allow the program to run correctly. If an Ubuntu program requires any additional system files, they will need to be installed separately, and will probably be available in packages of their own.

It's important to understand that *everything* in a typical Ubuntu installation originally came out of a package—from the Linux kernel, to the Nautilus file manager, to the system fonts. When you installed Ubuntu, the installation program did little more than unpack hundreds of packages in order.

APT and dpkg

Packages are installed and removed using Ubuntu's two software subsystems: the *Advanced Packaging Tool* (APT), and the *Debian Package* system (dpkg).

APT and dpkg are two sides of the same coin. dpkg works at a basic level doing the hard work of actually installing and removing packages, while APT works at a higher level keeping track of what packages are installed.

APT is very clever. Because it tracks everything, it will tell you if you try to install a software package that will cause trouble for an existing program. In most cases, it will even offer a solution.

Additionally, APT allows intelligent and efficient software updates—for both system software and applications.

Updating is possible because not only does the APT know what's already installed, but it also knows *what's available to be installed*, including newer versions of already-installed software. This is made possible through the use of *software repositories*.

Software repositories

It's with the use of software repositories that Ubuntu departs most radically from how Windows handles software management.

Repositories are large stores of packages. You might call them software libraries. Usually repositories are located online, but they can also be on CD/DVDs, or even a USB memory stick. The Ubuntu install CD is effectively a small repository, for example, containing only the software necessary for Ubuntu to be installed.

A typical Windows user will source software by downloading from a website or buying a CD/DVD-ROM disc. Virtually any software you might want to install on Ubuntu will probably be found in the software repositories. Therefore, installing new software is simply a matter of downloading and installing from the repositories.

APT handles both of these tasks automatically. As a user, you will not have to handle any package files directly.

The creation of such huge repositories of software is possible because practically all the software used under Ubuntu is *open source*. The source code—the original listing created by programmers—is available for everybody to use and appropriate however they wish. The Ubuntu developers take the source code for 1,000s of applications and create their own versions, tweaking the software if necessary so it works well under Ubuntu. Then they file it away in the repositories, ready for download and installation by end users.

> **NOTE** Because Linux software uses an open source approach, there often isn't an "official version" of some programs. For example, if you visit the Gnome website (www.gnome.org) and try to download binaries of the desktop software, you'll be told that you should search the repositories of your Linux distribution instead.

With Ubuntu it's unusual that a user will visit a website and manually download new software, although there is a notable exception: software that's so new it's not yet included in the official repositories. Many Ubuntu power-users often download such software.

> **NOTE** In many cases, to install cutting-edge software it's better to sign-up to the software developer's own personal repository. This is sometimes known as a *Personal Package Archive*, or PPA.

Out of the box, Ubuntu is signed up to several official repositories. These are listed in Table 6-1. You can add-in more repositories if you wish. This is useful when adding-in software that isn't officially supported. How to add repositories is explained in the *Working with Repositories* section later in this chapter.

Dependency management

Aside from the convenience (and luxury!) of having nearly all the world's Linux software just a download away, the use of repositories has another benefit: *dependency management*.

As mentioned earlier, a software package only contains the program itself. It doesn't contain any support software that might be needed, such as system libraries, or vital helper applications. They must be downloaded and installed separately, and are nearly always available in a package of their own.

Table 6-1. Default Ubuntu software repositories.

Repository	Details
Main	The Main repository is where core packages can be found. Essentially, this is the minimum repository needed to install Ubuntu from scratch, although several additional packages can also be found in Main that are non-essential to a fundamental setup. Software in Main is officially supported by Canonical, the sponsor of Ubuntu, so is guaranteed to be updated for the life of the particular release of Ubuntu.
Universe	Known as the "Community maintained" repository, this could also be referred to as "the rest", because it contains the majority of Free Software generated by the Linux community that isn't included in Main. Each package is maintained by members of the Ubuntu or Debian communities. The software in Universe isn't officially supported, so updates aren't guaranteed.
Restricted	Also known as "Proprietary drivers", this repository includes a small amount of non-open source software needed to make certain PC hardware work (mainly wireless and graphics devices). Software in this repository is regularly updated.
Multiverse	Known as "Software restricted by copyright or legal issues", this repository is effectively "the rest of the rest". Software found in Multiverse is incompatible with either the word or spirit of the Free Software license agreement used by Ubuntu. This doesn't necessarily mean software in Multiverse is proprietary, however. Multiverse software isn't officially supported and might not be updated.
Updates	Two update repositories are provided by which software fixes are made available; the "security" repository provides essential security updates, while the "updates" repository provides recommended updates.

If software needs additional packages to be installed, it is said to *depend* on the other packages. If the dependency packages aren't installed, the software just won't work. In fact, you won't even be allowed to install the software.

APT's job is to take care of dependencies, and it does so automatically and largely invisibly. It is aware of what a particular package requires and will automatically add any necessary packages to the tally for download and installation from the repositories.

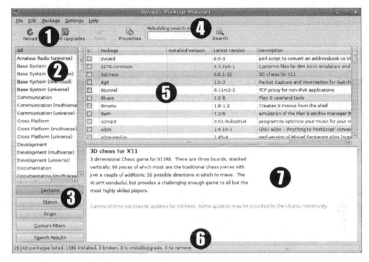

Figure 6-1. Synaptic Package Manager.

This applies the other way around too—should you try to uninstall some software that's depended upon by other software, APT will warn you and suggest a solution, such as removing the other software at the same time. Such packages are known as *reverse dependencies*.

Synaptic: An overview

You can add and remove software in two ways: using Synaptic Package Manager, which is a GUI tool, or at the command-line. Both are covered here, starting with Synaptic.

Synaptic can be found on the System ⇨ Administration menu. Its interface is easy to understand, and Figure 6-1 shows an annotated screenshot. Descriptions of the callouts are listed below. (Note that the screenshot is taken from Ubuntu 8.10; the version of Synaptic in Ubuntu 8.04 looks slightly different, but is largely identical.)

1. **Toolbar**: Here you can quickly access key functions of Synaptic. Perhaps the most useful buttons are RELOAD, that forces the computer to grab the latest list of packages in the repositories, and APPLY, that must be clicked to start installation/removal of software after selections have been made in the main package list.

TIP Some of the repositories are frequently updated, so you should always grab the latest lists from the repositories before installing new software. To this end, clicking the RELOAD button should be one of the first things you do each time upon starting Synaptic.

2. **Filter list**: This is where the filter selection appears (see Filters heading directly below). Clicking each entry in this list refines the main list of packages.

3. **Filters**: The buttons in the filter selection area let you select between collections of filters that are displayed in the filter list area above. The nature of each filter selection is marked on each button, and is described below:

    SECTIONS: This is the default view. Repositories are typically split into sections for easy browsing, and selecting the Sections filter list allows you to refine the main package list according to these sections. A description of the sections can be found at http://packages. ubuntu.com/intrepid/.

    STATUS: Here you can choose to filter the package list by those that are installed. Additionally, the "Not Installed (residual config)" option lets you filter by software that has been removed but whose configuration files are still present on the system.

    ORIGIN: This option lets you can filter the list of packages by individual repository. See Table 6-1 for a list of the default repositories.

    CUSTOM FILTERS: By clicking Settings ⇨ Filters you can create you own filters, typically to help repair problems within the software administration subsystems. Clicking the CUSTOM FILTERS button shows these filters, which include a list of readymade problem-solving filters.

    SEARCH RESULTS: This option is automatically selected whenever you search for a package.

4. **Search**: Ubuntu 8.10 offers various methods of searching for packages, and two are found here on the toolbar (Synaptic as supplied with Ubuntu 8.04 only shows the single SEARCH button). By typing into the Quick Search field, you can quickly search package names and descriptions. Alternatively, you can click the SEARCH button and perform a more thorough search.

5. **Main package list**: This is where the list of available packages appears. If no filter is applied, *all* packages from *all* repositories are listed (some 26,135 packages with Ubuntu 8.10!). Packages with an Ubuntu icon besides them are officially supported, which is to say they will be updated for the life of the particular release of Ubuntu you're using. To install a package, click the checkbox alongside it. Packages already installed have their checkboxes colored green, and clicking the checkbox will let you mark the package for removal. For a list of all possible checkbox states, click Help ⇨ Icon Legend.

6. **Status bar**: Here you can view summaries of the number of packages displayed in the main package list, along with details of how many are installed, are broken (i.e. do not have dependencies installed—see later), and how many are marked to be installed, removed or upgraded.

7. **Package description**: A full description of the currently selected package appears here. Beneath each description is a note about the nature of updates (Ubuntu 8.10 and above only).

Typical tasks

Let's stroll through some typical software management tasks.

Installing software

Frozen-Bubble (www.frozen-bubble.org) is an excellent clone of the classic Bust-a-Move video game. Not only is it fun to play, but it's a good example of the quality of games available for Linux.

The steps needed to install it are described below. The same steps apply in order to identify and install any software package in the repositories:

1. Start Synaptic (System ⇨ Administration ⇨ Synaptic Package Manager). Before installing any software, you should always grab the latest list of packages from the repositories. This means hitting the RELOAD button on the main toolbar.

2. Hit the SEARCH button on the toolbar. In the Search field, type frozen bubble and click the dialog box's SEARCH button.

3. After a few seconds a list of packages will appear. Some of these packages will be support packages for Frozen-Bubble, and some might be entirely irrelevant, so common sense is needed to

ensure you choose the package for the actual program. Selecting each of the packages and reading the descriptions should be sufficient, and it should become obvious that the package needed to install the program is called `frozen-bubble`.

> **TIP** If you already know the specific package name (maybe you read it on a web page, for example), a quicker method of searching is to ensure a package is selected in the main list, and to simply start typing the package name. This will automatically filter the list of packages according to what you type.

4. Click the checkbox alongside the `frozen-bubble` entry in the list. Immediately, you will see a pop-up menu offering a variety of options. The one needed for installation is Mark for Installation.

5. Once you've made your selection, a dialog may appear explaining that additional packages need to be installed. These are the dependencies required for the program to work correctly. You should click the MARK button to add them to the list of packages to be installed. If you click CANCEL instead, the original package will be deselected.

> **NOTE** While nearly all programs have dependencies, it's not always the case that you will be prompted to install them, because they may already be installed on the system. If you don't see a prompt to install dependencies then don't worry—it's unlikely anything has gone wrong.

6. Now click the APPLY button on the toolbar. A summary dialog box will appear showing the packages that are to be installed (click the SHOW DETAILS button to see the complete list). Additionally, you'll be told how much disk space the new application will take up. Assuming you're happy with all of this, click the APPLY button in the dialog box to install the software.

Download and installation takes place automatically, usually in a matter of minutes. A confirmation dialog will appear at the end and, following this, you will find an icon for the new software on the relevant Applications or System submenu—in the case of Frozen-Bubble, the icon appears on the Applications ⇨ Games menu.

> **TIP** In addition to dependencies, some packages have a list of recommended packages, and sometimes a list of suggested packages too. These are non-essential add-ons that enhance the program's features. For example, if you install a word processor, a thesaurus application might be a suggested package. You can install the recommended and/or suggested packages by

right-clicking the package and selecting from the Mark Recommended and/or Mark Suggested submenus.

Uninstalling software

Removing a software package is just as easy as installing it. Use Synaptic's search function to find the relevant package (search by the program name, as when installing software), and click the checkbox alongside the program's package in the list.

A menu will pop-up offering a variety of options, as follows:

Mark for Reinstallation: This will refresh the software, as described in the section below.

Mark for Removal: This will remove the software, but leave behind its configuration files so that the software will function in the same way should you decide to install it again at a future date. This is the best choice.

Mark for Complete Removal: This will remove the software and also delete its configuration files.

Assuming you make a selection to remove the software, a cross will appear in the checkbox. When you click the APPLY button on the main toolbar, you'll once again see a summary of the actions that are to be performed. Click APPLY in the dialog box to continue.

Removing a software package doesn't remove any dependencies that were installed along with it. That presently isn't possible using Synaptic, although it is possible at the command-line, as described in the *Command-Line Software Management* section below.

> **NOTE** Sometimes you might see a heading in the Summary dialog that reads Unchanged. This indicates software packages for which updates are available. I explain more about updating in Chapter 7, but if you wish to install updates using Synaptic you can click the MARK ALL UPGRADES button on the toolbar.

Reinstalling software

Sometimes software installed on the system might become corrupted, in which case it might not run, or might function incorrectly. In such a case it can be useful to reinstall the software, and Synaptic offers a method of doing so. Search for the program's package and click the checkbox alongside it. In the menu that appears, click the Mark for Reinstallation option, and click the APPLY button on the main toolbar.

After confirming what it's about to do via the Summary dialog box (just like when installing/removing software), Synaptic will run through the procedures of installing the software, such as unpacking the package and configuring the software, but without actually downloading it afresh *unless* the package file isn't stored in the package cache, in which case it will have to be downloaded from the repositories.

Manually installing a package

It is inadvisable you attempt to manually download a package and install it. The process is fraught with problems, the most significant being the potential difficulty in manually sourcing dependencies.

> **NOTE** Because of dependency issues, if you intend to install software found on a developer's website, you'll probably find that the developer has her own package repository that you can subscribe to. This will let you use Synaptic to install the program, thus taking care of dependencies automatically. Adding a new repository is described in the *Working with Repositories* section below.

However, there are a handful of situations where installing a package "by hand" might be required.

The GDebi Package Installer program automatically associates with package files (they have a .deb extension), in the same way that OpenOffice.org's Writer associates with Microsoft Word .doc files. Therefore, manually installing a package is simply a matter of downloading the package file and double-clicking it, or more simply, selecting the Open with GDebi Package Installer option in the web browser's download dialog box.

GDebi attempts to mitigate any dependency issues by downloading the necessary dependency packages from the main repositories. However, you shouldn't assume the dependency packages will always be available, particularly if you are installing a package that isn't built specifically for the release of Ubuntu you're using.

Once the GDebi program window appears, click the INSTALL PACKAGES button. Following this, any dependencies will be downloaded (if possible) and the software installed.

If any required dependencies can't be found in the repositories, the INSTALL PACKAGE button will be grayed out, and a warning will appear telling you the names of the missing dependencies. You will have to manually source and install the dependency packages before continuing.

Table 6-2. Typical software administration commands (apt top, dpkg bottom).

Command	Details
apt-get update	Update the list of available software from the repositories (equivalent to Synaptic's RELOAD button, and, as such, should be used before any software installation).
apt-cache search searchterm	Search the repositories for *searchterm*. The specific name of matching packages along with summary descriptions will be returned.
apt-cache show packagename	Show details of *packagename*, including what dependencies it has, and its full description.
apt-get install packagename	Install *packagename*. Any dependencies will be automatically added to the list, and you'll be asked to confirm the total install tally. Multiple packages can be specified.
apt-get autoremove packagename	Uninstall *packagename*, along with any *unused* dependencies. To uninstall only the specified package, and leave dependencies in place, use apt-get remove *packagename*. If issued without specifying a package, apt-get autoremove will attempt to remove all redundant dependency packages on the system.
apt-get upgrade	Update to the latest versions of installed software.
apt-get dist-upgrade	Effectively, this command upgrades the entire system to the newest release of Ubuntu.
apt-get clean	Clears the package cache; useful if disk space is tight, but otherwise not necessary.
dpkg -i *packagename*.deb	Manually install the file *packagename*.deb, assuming you have manually downloaded it.
dpkg -r *packagename*	Uninstall *packagename*; it is necessary to specify the package name as it's known on the system (i.e. within Synaptic), rather than the package filename, as required for installation.
dpkg -P *packagename*	Uninstall *packagename*, also removing its configuration files.
dpkg -I *packagename*.deb	Show information about *packagename*.deb, including full description and dependencies.
dpkg -l *packagename*	List details of installed package called *packagename*, including version number.

NOTE Bear in mind that dependencies typically have their *own* dependencies! In other words, it's likely that you'll source all the dependencies needed by the program, only to be presented with an entirely new list! This situation is known as "dependency hell", and is the main reason why APT was invented.

Packages that have been manually installed can be removed using Synaptic, just like any other software.

Command-line software management

As useful as it is, Synaptic is little more than a graphical front-end for a series of commands that administer the APT software subsystem.

The two most useful commands are apt-get and apt-cache. In addition to these commands, it is possible to install packages you've manually downloaded using the dpkg command.

Installing software at the command-line can be quicker and more efficient than using Synaptic, so is a skill worth learning.

NOTE Of course, command-line software installation is also possible if the GUI isn't working. It can therefore be very useful when trying to repair a broken system.

In the sections below, I look at the same common software installation tasks mentioned previously, but this time at the command-line.

For those who want a quick start, the most useful subset of software administration commands are outlined in Table 6-2. Remember that software installation requires root powers, so each software install or remove command should be preceded with sudo (commands that search or display information do not usually require root powers).

TIP Some people prefer to use the aptitude command instead of the APT commands. aptitude is slightly better in how it handles dependencies, and features a semi-GUI interface that makes it easy to use. For more details, see http://algebraicthunk.net/~dburrows/projects/aptitude/doc/en/.

Installing software

Here are the steps required to install the Frozen-Bubble game, as discussed previously.

1. The first command to type before installing any software is sudo apt-get update. This will grab the latest list of software from the repositories.

2. The apt-cache search command can be used to search through the list of available software. To search for Frozen-Bubble, something similar to the following could be typed:

- apt-cache search frozen bubble

Here's what I see on my test system:

```
fb-music-high - High quality, large music files for  ♂
Frozen-Bubble
fb-music-low - Lower quality, small music files for  ♂
Frozen-Bubble
frozen-bubble - Pop out the bubbles!
frozen-bubble-data - Data files for Frozen-Bubble
pengupop - Online multiplayer clone of Bust a Move
```

3. To view complete details about any package, use the apt-cache show command; for example:

- apt-cache show frozen-bubble

The information provided can scroll off the screen so it's often useful to pipe it into the less text viewer, for easy reading (i.e. apt-cache show frozen-bubble|less).

4. Once you've found the name of the correct package, the apt-get install command can be used to install it; installing software requires root powers, so the command must be preceded with sudo:

- sudo apt-get install frozen-bubble

If no dependencies are required, the package will be downloaded and installed instantly. If dependencies are required, which is likely, they will automatically be added to the list of files to be downloaded and installed. A summary will be shown to which you can type Y, to agree, or N, to cancel software installation.

Assuming you agree, the software will be downloaded and installed. Progress will be displayed as it happens.

Sometimes certain system configuration tasks might be carried out during the installation of software packages. For example, if you choose to install a new package containing fonts, the system font caches will probably be refreshed. Such tasks happen automatically and, if Synaptic is used, are usually hidden from view. However, when installing at the command-line you'll see each task complete. Usually there is nothing about which to be concerned. If any administrative task has even the possibility of damaging the system, or changing a vital setting, you'll be prompted to confirm that you wish it to run.

Uninstalling software

Removing software is just as easy as installing software, and all you need is the name of the package. If you've forgotten what this is, you can once again use apt-cache search to find it.

Following this, use the apt-get autoremove command—the following will uninstall Frozen-Bubble:

- sudo apt-get autoremove frozen-bubble

You'll be shown a list of the packages to be removed (that will include any redundant dependencies), and asked to confirm your decision by hitting Y or N.

> **NOTE** Only *unused dependencies* will be marked for removal. This might vary from the list of dependencies that were originally installed. This disparity occurs because other software you've installed since also requires the dependencies.

Reinstalling software

To refresh a package that's already installed, type the following, replacing *packagename* with the name of the program as it is listed in Synaptic or via apt-cache search:

- sudo apt-get --reinstall install *packagename*

If the package isn't already present in the system's package cache (located at /var/cache/apt/archives), it will be downloaded afresh.

Manually installing/uninstalling packages

If you find yourself having to install a package manually, the dpkg command can be used. The -i command option is used to install and the -r option can be used to remove packages, as follows:

- sudo dpkg -i *packagename.deb*
- sudo dpkg -r *packagename*

> **NOTE** Once a package is installed using dpkg, it can also be removed using the apt-get autoremove command.

The full filename of the package file must be specified when installing.

This isn't necessary for removal of the software. Instead, you need only refer to the package by its "short name"—how it appears in the list of packages provided by Synaptic or apt-cache search.

TIP The short name is usually the first part of the package's filename.

To see the full description contained in a downloaded package file, that includes a list of the dependencies it requires, use the -I command option (pipe the output to less because otherwise it will scroll off the screen):

- dpkg -I *packagename*.deb|less

To see if a package is installed—useful for checking if the required dependencies for a package are met—use the -l command option with dpkg (that's lower-case L), and specify the package's short name. If the package isn't installed, you will see "No packages found". If it is installed you will see a table showing the package version number and sundry details.

Installation limitations

Because of dependency issues, restrictions are placed on how dpkg works when installing/removing software. This protects the system from damage.

If you attempt to install a package that requires dependencies that aren't already installed, you'll be told what they are. The software will then be installed but *won't be configured for use*. This means that, essentially, the program files are in place, but any vital system tweaks necessary for the program to work correctly haven't been carried out.

A package installed without dependencies is known as a *broken package*. Installing a broken package will leave the package management system in a damaged state; apt-get will refuse to work until the dependencies are met or the errant package is uninstalled, while Synaptic will automatically insist on removing the package before allowing any further package installation.

TIP If the dependency packages are available in the repositories, it's possible to fix the situation at the command-line by typing sudo apt-get -f install. This will download the dependencies, install them, and configure the broken package for use.

Uninstallation limitations

If you attempt to use dpkg to uninstall a package that is a dependency of other packages, you simply won't be allowed. Instead, you'll be told what other programs depend on that package, and you must manually remove them first (of course, it's likely they will have their own dependencies, giving rise to another "dependency hell" situation).

Working with repositories

As an Ubuntu user you're not limited to the official repositories. Many third parties offer their own repositories, and you can sign-up to as many as you wish.

The benefits of signing up to a third-party repository are that you can install any software contained in the repository via Synaptic or apt-get. Additionally, if a new version of the software becomes available, you will be notified automatically via Ubuntu's Update Manager, and will be able to install the new version alongside system updates.

Adding a repository

To add a new repository, all you need is the address. This looks like an extended web address. For example, here's the repository address provided by Skype, the people behind the VoIP telephone communications software:

```
deb http://download.skype.com/linux/repos/debian/ stable ⏎
non-free
```

To add a new repository address to the system, follow these steps:

1. Start the Software Sources program (it can be found in the System ⇨ Administration menu), and click the Third Party Software tab in the window that appears.

2. Click the ADD button and, in the APT Line field, type the *whole* address line, including the deb component at the beginning of the line, and any words at the end (it would make sense to copy and paste if it's on a web page).

3. Once done, click the ADD SOURCE button, and the CLOSE button in the parent window. You'll be prompted to update the list of software contained in the repositories, so do so.

It should be noted that the Software Sources program merely adds the address you enter to the /etc/apt/sources.list file. Therefore, to add a repository at the command-line, you need only edit this file and add the new repository line at the end. Then perform a refresh of the repository lists (sudo apt-get update).

Adding a new repository key

Sometimes a repository contains *digitally signed* packages. Signing is a method of ensuring packages haven't been tampered with, or forged. The programmer stamps each package with an ID that only she can create. This is done using a cryptographic key, the public component of which is offered for download and must be installed by end users.

You can add the public key to your system in the following way:

1. The key is usually offered for download at the same place you'll find the package—it will have an .asc or .gpg file extension. Right-click it and select Save As, then save it to disk. Be sure to download the key only from the package creator's website, and not a mirror site. After all, it's possible the key may also have been tampered with.

2. In the Software Sources program, click the Authentication tab and click the IMPORT KEY FILE button. Then navigate to the file you saved. Click OK when done.

To import the key at the command-line, type the following, replacing *keyfile.gpg* with the name of the downloaded file:

- sudo apt-key add *keyfile.gpg*

  NOTE If the packages you attempt to install come from a third party repository and *aren't* digitally signed, you may see a warning during installation saying the packages can't be authenticated. This is there to warn you that you're installing non-official packages, but is usually nothing to worry about.

Compiling from source code

The nature of Linux means that virtually all available software is *open source*—the source code is free for people to view, use, and even adapt into new software.

In the heyday of Unix back in the 1970s/80s, the *only* method of installing new software was to take the source code and *compile* it—manually turn it into a *binary* that can be run day-to-day.

Although ready-made and pre-compiled software packages rule the roost when it comes to Ubuntu software installation, you may find some Linux software is only available as source code. This is often the case with new hardware drivers that must be manually compiled in order to work correctly with the kernel program.

Before attempting to compile software yourself, use Synaptic to install the build-essential package. This installs the necessary program compilation software.

Three commands are commonly used in succession to compile software, once you've unpacked the source code and switched into the folder containing it:

- `./configure`
- `make`
- `sudo make install`

The first command runs a script that checks the system has the required software needed to compile the software, and also any dependency software required to eventually run the program.

The second command actually compiles the software, and as such can take quite a while to complete. The screen may seem to fill with garbage during this stage. This is *debug output*, and is nothing to be worried about, although if you run into problems when compiling software and ask for help online, others may ask to see it.

The third command copies the newly-made program files to the relevant locations in the filesystem, so they're ready for everyday use.

It's beyond the scope of this pocket guide to explain software compilation in more depth than this but, bearing in mind this is the most fundamental (and oldest) of Unix tasks, you'll find excellent instructions online—just hit your favorite search engine.

CHAPTER SEVEN

Securing the system

This chapter looks at five aspects of system configuration that help increase Ubuntu's security. They are:

- Updating the system;
- Configuring the firewall to protect your computer from network/Internet threats;
- Installing an antivirus program;
- Encrypting data, so that even if your data is stolen or misplaced it will be inaccessible;
- Enhancing security within your web browser.

System updates

As with any operating system, you should regularly update Ubuntu. This will ensure you have the latest software that's free of bugs and security holes that make your system insecure by providing a backdoor for hackers or viruses.

Update Manager

Ubuntu automates updating the system using a program called Update Manager. This runs periodically and automatically in the background to check for updated versions of installed software that have been made available in the repositories.

You may already have noticed this program's icon appearing in the notification area—depending on the GUI theme in use, it looks like a star, or red down-pointing arrow, and the first time it appears a callout will appear informing you that updates are available.

Clicking the icon will show a list of packages that can be updated.

> **TIP** Ensure any other software installation application is closed first, such as Synaptic. Only one software administration tool can run at any one time. This includes command-line tools.

It's not absolutely essential to read through the list of updates, but doing so will only take a minute or two, and it's a good idea to keep track of what's being updated. Assuming you're happy with the list of updates, click the INSTALL UPDATES button to automatically download and install the software.

If desired, you can force Update Manager to run by clicking its entry on the System ⇨ Administration menu and clicking the CHECK button when the program window appears.

Depending on what system components are updated, you may have to restart your computer to complete installation. You'll know if this is the case because the update manager icon will change to two circular arrows that, when clicked, will prompt you to reboot the computer.

When a new release of Ubuntu becomes available, Update Manager will inform you via a pop-up window. You can then choose to upgrade (or not, if you do not wish to).

Updating at the command-line

To update at the command-line, two sets of commands can be issued:

- sudo apt-get update
- sudo apt-get upgrade

or

- sudo apt-get update
- sudo apt-get dist-upgrade

sudo apt-get update grabs the latest list of packages, so should always be used before updating.

sudo apt-get upgrade updates all software packages to the latest available versions. If you wish to update the system manually at the command-line, this command should be issued weekly. In contrast, sudo apt-get dist-upgrade updates the entire system, including several vital system files, and thereby updates Ubuntu to the latest release. If run on an 8.04 system, for example, it will update Ubuntu to 8.10. It should be run only when you know a new release to be available.

Configuring the firewall

Ubuntu contains a very powerful firewall called *netfilter* that is part of the central kernel program. However, it isn't active by default, and must be manually configured. The reason for this is that Ubuntu has no *outward-facing services.* If you imagine Ubuntu as a house, you could say that it has no windows or doors through which intruders can gain access. All incoming connections hit a brick wall.

However, despite this fundamental protection, hackers are ingenious and there can be no room for complacency. Configuring the firewall using a GUI application like Firestarter, as described below, is so easy that there's little reason not to do so.

> **TIP** The ufw command can be used to configure the firewall at the command-line. This is relatively simple to use, but is still not as straightforward as a GUI application like Firestarter. For more details, see http://ubuntuforums.org/showthread.php?t=823741.

Installing and configuring Firestarter

Firestarter is a simple yet powerful firewall configuration tool. To install it, start Synaptic and search for firestarter. Put a check in the box alongside the firestarter entry in the results list and select Mark for Installation from the menu that appears. Click the APPLY button on the toolbar, and the APPLY button in the dialog box that appears.

There's no need to restart because Ubuntu's firewall component can be started, stopped and reconfigured while the system is up and running. However, it is necessary to complete an initial wizard to configure Firestarter itself, so start the program by clicking System ⇨ Administration ⇨ Firestarter to run through this.

> **NOTE** Bear in mind that there's no reason to have the Firestarter configuration program running to enjoy the protection of Ubuntu's firewall. All Firestarter does is configure Ubuntu's built-in firewall. It isn't a firewall application in itself.

Click the FORWARD button to work through the wizard. When asked to select the network device you wish to protect, select the connection type from the Detected Device(s) dropdown list. If you're using a wireless connection, ensure the list reads Wireless Device, or similar (see Figure 7-1). Bear in mind that "Ethernet" refers to a wired connection, wherein the computer is connected by cable to a router, switch, or hub.

Leave the other options as they are and click FORWARD to work through the wizard to completion. At the end, click the SAVE button.

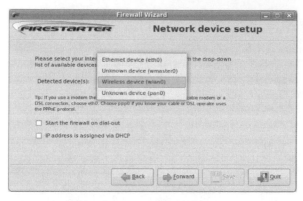

Figure 7-1. Firestarter configuration.

In its default state, Firestarter turns-away all incoming data, while all out-going data is permitted through the firewall. As such, it is little different from the default Ubuntu state of affairs.

NOTE On a technical level, Firestarter works by letting you allow and deny individual TCP/UDP ports. There's not really any need to understand this to configure Firestarter, but it will certainly help if you want to create more elaborate arrangements. Many websites offer explanations of how TCP and ports work—just hit Google.

Two types of rules can be created: *inbound rules*, that allow through connections from the network or Internet, and *outbound rules*, that can block unauthorized data emissions from your computer, such as those from potential virus infections, or spyware.

NOTE There are almost no viruses or spyware infestations affecting Linux. However, this is almost certain to change as versions of Linux like Ubuntu become more popular.

Creating inbound rules

Inbound rules allow you to filter all incoming connections. By default, all incoming connections are turned away. Creating an inbound rule effectively allows you to create a "hole" in the firewall for certain types of connection to get through, as needed by particular programs. This can be useful if you run file sharing software on your computer, for example, such as Transmission (Applications ⇨ Internet), that uses BitTorrent to share files.

Additionally, you can choose to let some inbound connections through, but only if they originate on the local network (i.e. within a particular IP address range). This can be useful in the case of shared folders, for example, where other computers in your workplace or home may wish to access files on your computer.

Here are the steps required to create an in-bound rule:

1. Start the Firestarter configuration program, if it isn't already running, by clicking System ⇨ Administration ⇨ Firestarter. You'll need to type your password when prompted.

2. Click the Policy tab in the program window, and ensure Inbound Traffic Policy is selected in the Editing dropdown list.

3. Under the Allow Service heading in the lower-half of the program window, right-click and select Add Rule from the menu that appears.

4. In the dialog box that appears, select from the Name dropdown list the type or program that you'd like to allow through the firewall. For example, to allow BitTorrent connections, select that in the list. To let others access shared folders on your computer, select Samba (SMB). Note that the Port field will be automatically filled in once you make your selection. You can edit this if you wish, but there should be no need.

5. If the rule relates to inbound connections from the Internet, ensure the Anyone radio button is selected under the When The Source Is heading.

6. To limit the type of incoming connection to the local network, and not the entire Internet, click the IP, Host or Network radio button. You'll then need to find out the network range that your computer is part of. To do so, right-click the NetworkManager icon at the top-right of the screen, and select Connection Information. Look in the IP Address line within the dialog box that appears, and make a note of the first three numbers. On my test PC, this line read 192.168.1.5, so I made a note of 192.168.1.

7. Back in Firestarter's rule creation dialog box, type the numbers, followed by a period, then a zero. So, in my case I typed 192.168.1.0. Then add a forward slash, and type 24. On my test PC the entire line read 192.168.1.0/24.

8. Once done, click the ADD button, and then the APPLY POLICY button on the toolbar. Then close Firestarter.

9. However, if you're adding a rule to allow access to Samba shared folders on the computer, another step is necessary to let other computers "see" the shared resources across the network. Click Edit ⇨ Preferences within Firestarter and, on the left of the dialog box that appears, click the Advanced Options entry in the list. Remove the check from Block Broadcast From External Network. Click ACCEPT when done.

The new rule will take effect immediately. To delete it at a later stage, start Firestarter, right-click the rule, and click Remove Rule. Then click the APPLY POLICY button.

Creating outbound rules

When it comes to blocking data emanating from your computer, Firestarter can enact two different modes: *whitelist*, and *blacklist*.

Whitelist: In this mode, network traffic is not allowed out of the computer unless a rule allows it. This is also known as a *restrictive policy*.

Blacklist: In this mode, which is default, all traffic is allowed out of the computer unless a rule specifically forbids it. This is also known as a *permissive policy*.

Whitelist mode undoubtedly offers the most secure protection, but at the expense of having to create a rule for each type of outbound connection you're likely to make. You will need to make individual rules for connections emanating from all the software on your system: web, email, instant messaging, and so on.

> **NOTE** You will need to create two rules for web connections: one for standard HTTP, and another for HTTPS secure connections, such as those used by online shops, banks and email services. Additionally, some websites insist on using non-standard port numbers, in which case they will be blocked to you unless you create a custom rule allowing that particular port.

You can switch between the modes by clicking the Policy tab in the Firestarter window, selecting Outbound Traffic Policy from the Editing dropdown list, and clicking the radio button alongside either entry.

Here's how to create an outbound rule regardless of what policy you decide upon:

1. Ensure the Policy tab is selected within Firestarter and right-click beneath the Deny Service (or Allow Service) heading near the bottom of the program window. In the menu that appears, select Add Rule.

2. As when creating rules, select the type of connection you'd like to allow/deny from the Name dropdown list. Ignore the sections beneath the When The Source Is heading—they are only for use if Firestarter is managing Internet connection sharing on your computer.

3. To create a custom rule for a particular port number, manually type a name of your own choosing into the Name field (although this is a dropdown list you can still type within it), and type the port number into the Port box.

> **TIP** If you've opted for a whitelist (restrictive) policy, at the very least you should create individual rules for HTTP, HTTPS, POP3, and SMTP. For a complete list of popular TCP/IP ports, that you can use to create additional rules, see http://en.wikipedia.org/wiki/Port_number.

4. When done, click the ADD button, and the APPLY POLICY button on the main toolbar. Then close Firestarter.

The new rule takes effect immediately. To delete a rule at a later stage, right-click it and select Remove Rule. Then click APPLY POLICY.

Turning off diagnostic tool responses

There's an additional step you can take to protect your computer from potential Internet threats: turning off responses to diagnostic tools. However, this will mean you won't be able to "ping" your computer. This can be useful when diagnosing network problems.

To turn off diagnostic tool responses, click Edit ⇨ Preferences in Firestarter's main program window, select ICMP Filtering from the list on the left of the dialog box that appears, and put a check in Enable ICMP Filtering. *Don't put a check in any of the boxes beneath this!* Once done, click the ACCEPT button, then click the APPLY POLICY button in the main toolbar, and close the Firestarter program.

Installing antivirus

Many people say using an antivirus program with Ubuntu is not necessary. It's hard to argue. There are practically no viruses or malware for Linux at the present time. There's some debate about whether this will change in future, but right now an Ubuntu user is quite simply safe from viruses. No further action is required.

However, aside from guarding against future threats, installing an antivirus program allows you to watch out for Windows or even Mac viruses in files sent to you. Therefore, you can avoid passing on virus-infected files that might affect those running non-Linux operating systems.

> **TIP** Why not convert your friends or colleagues to using Ubuntu? The fact Ubuntu is immune to viruses is a very persuasive argument in its favor. If you do convert them, be sure to suggest they get a copy of *Ubuntu Pocket Guide and Reference* to help them get started!

There is a variety of commercially sold antivirus programs for Linux, but perhaps the best choice from an open source perspective is ClamAV. This is industrial-strength antivirus designed for server computers, but you can also install ClamTK, a small program that provides a graphical front end, and thereby makes ClamAV suitable for more humble users.

Installing ClamTK

Start Synaptic and search for `clamtk`. Put a check alongside the `clamtk` entry in the results, and click Mark for Installation in the menu that appears. Agree to install the list of dependencies, that includes ClamAV itself, and then click the APPLY button on the toolbar.

When ClamTK is run for the first time it's necessary to update the virus database. In future this will be done automatically and periodically in the background, without any need for user intervention.

To manually update the database, ClamTK needs to run as root user, so open a terminal window (Applications ⇨ Accessories ⇨ Terminal), and type the following:

- `gksu clamtk`

Click Help ⇨ Update Signatures. Once ClamTK reports the signatures are up to date, close the program window.

> **TIP** You can update the virus database at the command-line by typing `sudo freshclam`. Don't worry if, while doing this, you see a warning that ClamAV is out-of-date—this simply means that the version offered in the Ubuntu repositories is lagging a little behind the main releases. This is not an issue.

Scanning for viruses

To start ClamTK, click Applications ⇨ System Tools ⇨ Virus Scanner.

It's not a good idea to scan the entire filesystem using ClamTK, because ClamAV simply isn't built for that task. In fact, in my tests, any attempt to do a full filesystem scan caused ClamAV/TK to crash.

Therefore, you should limit scans to your /home folder. This is where virus-infected files are most likely to be found because it's where most files you download will end-up.

> **NOTE** If you're worried about getting a virus when installing software, don't be. All software in the Ubuntu repositories is digitally signed. This is a method of ensuring the files can't be tampered with. It's true that any software packages you manually download and install might contain viruses, but it's very unlikely.

Before starting a scan, ensure that ClamAV scans hidden files by clicking Options ⇨ Scan Hidden Files (.*).

To start a scan of your /home folder, click File ⇨ Home (Thorough). If using Ubuntu 8.04, click File ⇨ Full Home Scan.

Any virus-infected files found will be listed under the File heading in the ClamTK program window, along with their location (path). The type of virus infection will be listed under the Status heading.

You may see other files listed in the results area after a scan. If a file was too big to scan, it will be listed. If you wish to have ClamAV scan all files, regardless of size, click Options ⇨ No Maximum Size. Bear in mind this may dramatically increase the time taken to scan.

ClamAV is unable to remove any virus infections found in a file. Instead, the user must decide the course of action to take. Usually, deleting the file is best.

All antivirus programs are prone to *false positives*—identifying files as containing viruses when they don't. To guard against this, should ClamAV report what it thinks is an infected file, search Google, specifying the name of the file and the name of the virus. If one or more people have encountered a similar result, that can help identify a false alarm.

Encrypting files and folders

Encryption is a method of encoding files so that they can't be accessed without first being decoded. This usually requires a passphrase.

The goal of encryption is usually to stop unauthorized individuals accessing private data. You might choose to encrypt personal files, for example, such as bank statements. Or you might choose to encrypt a file while transferring it across the Internet, so anybody who intercepts it in transit will be unable to read it.

Ubuntu allows the encryption and decryption of files and folders, but those using Ubuntu 8.10 or later can also create an encrypted file store, in which files are automatically and invisibly encrypted.

Creating an encrypted /private folder

Ubuntu 8.10 Intrepid Ibex introduces technology that allows on-the-fly encryption of files.

How it works is that an encrypted filestore is created. This is effectively a large archive file, like a tar file.

When the user logs in, the filestore is "unlocked" and mounted in the /private folder within a user's /home folder.

Any files saved to /private are automatically encrypted, although the user is entirely unaware of this. They can browse the folder just like any other, and read/write files within it without any additional work. If a file is removed from the folder, it is automatically decrypted but, again, this is invisible to the user.

Nobody apart from the owner is able to access the files within the /private folder—other users are locked out, although the root user can access the files while the user is logged in.

When the user logs out, or shuts down the computer, the filestore is "locked"—the filestore is unmounted, making its contents inaccessible until the next login. This stops anybody accessing the files by booting the computer into rescue mode—a common way of bypassing security measures, in which the user is given root powers without having to enter a password.

Setting-up the encrypted folder is simple. First, if you haven't already, update your system software as described at the beginning of this chapter. Then open a terminal window (Applications ⇨ Accessories ⇨ Terminal) and type the following commands:

- `sudo apt-get install ecryptfs-utils`
- `ecryptfs-setup-private`

You'll need to type your login password when prompted after typing the second of the commands. You'll also be invited to create a mount passphrase. This can be anything from a few words to a sentence, and can include numbers and symbols such as punctuation marks. Ensure you remember what you type because you might need it at a future date to manually unlock the filestore! Alternatively, you can simply hit Enter to have a passphrase generated automatically, but you should print out the passphrase and store it in a secure location.

Once the commands have completed, log out and back in again.

When the desktop appears, you'll find you have a new /private folder within your /home folder. As mentioned, this can be used just like a standard folder—files and folders can be stored there, and you will see no sign that the contents of the folder are in fact encrypted.

> **NOTE** The third-party TrueCrypt software (www.truecrypt.org) allows you to create encrypted filestores on *any version* of Ubuntu, not just 8.10. My book *Ubuntu Kung Fu* explains how to use TrueCrypt and I've reproduced the TrueCrypt section on the book's website: visit www.ubuntukungfu.org/truecrypt.html.

Encrypting individual files and folders

Users of both Ubuntu 8.04 and 8.10 can encrypt individual files and folders. This is unrelated to encryption of the /private folder.

Here's how this feature is typically used. Usually, a user encrypts a file, creating an encrypted copy. She then permanently deletes the original. If the user wishes to access the file again, she must decrypt the file. If the file is subsequently changed by editing, it must be re-encrypted afresh.

As you might guess, this type of encryption is best for files that you won't access frequently, such as old files you wish to archive.

It makes use of public/private key cryptography. This is primarily used to encrypt email, but it can also be used to encrypt files.

> **NOTE** The way key pair encryption works means encryption/decryption is limited to computers on which the key pair is installed. So, this isn't an ideal way of creating encrypted files you wish to share with others.

Creating a key pair

To encrypt and decrypt files, first you'll need to create a key pair, as follows (this is a task you only need do once):

1. Start the Password and Encryption Keys program. It's on the Applications ⇨ Accessories menu.

2. Click the NEW button at the bottom of the program window. In the dialog box that appears, select PGP Key, and click CONTINUE.

3. Enter personal details, as requested. These details are relevant only if you intend to use the key pair to encrypt emails. If creating keys simply for personal encryption purposes, any details can be filled in, although note that you need to type a first and last name in the Full Name field. When done, click the CREATE button.

4. Enter a passphrase. This is what you'll need to type to decrypt any files you encrypt, so it's important you choose something memorable. It should also be as long as possible, and hard to guess. Spaces and symbols can be used. Enter the passphrase twice to confirm correct typing—once in the Password text field, and once in the Confirm field. Click OK when done.

NOTE *Do not forget the passphrase*! If it is lost, any data you have encrypted is also lost. There is no way of recovering the data, and no way of cracking the encryption. Ubuntu uses 2,048-bit encryption keys. It is theorized that to crack such a key would take more time than the universe has been in existence!

5. Following this, the keys are created. This can take some time, depending on your PC's speed. Once it's finished, click to close the Passwords and Encryption Keys program window.

Encrypting a file or folder

To encrypt a file or folder, simply right-click it and select Encrypt from the menu that appears. In the dialog box put a check alongside the key you created (there will probably only be one option), and click OK.

If encrypting a folder, you'll be asked if you want to encrypt each file in the folder separately, or package them all together in an archive. The latter is the best option, and you'll be asked to choose the archive type you want to use (i.e. .zip, .tar.gz etc.). The choice of compression format makes no difference to the encryption.

Once done, you'll find a new file alongside the original file or folder, with the same filename, but with an additional .pgp file extension. This is the encrypted version of the file or folder. If you chose to encrypt a folder and create an archive, the archive file will also be present.

The original file (and archive, if applicable) should be deleted.

TIP To permanently delete a file or folder, rather than send it to the trash where it might be recovered, click it once and type Shift+Delete. Alternatively, delete it at the command-line. For extra security, use the shred command. This not only deletes files, but also destroys any "residue" left on the disk by overwriting the data. To use it, just type shred -u *filename*, replacing *filename* with the name of the file.

Decrypting a file or folder

To decrypt a .pgp file, simply double-click it. You'll be prompted to type the passphrase you created during key production, so do so. You should now find the original file (or archive) is visible alongside the .pgp file.

Remember that it is only possible to decrypt a file on a computer on which the relevant encryption keys are installed. Usually this is the computer on which the keys were generated, unless the keys have been exported, as described in the following section.

Exporting a key pair for use on another PC

It's a wise idea to backup your encryption keys because, without them, there is quite simply no way of decrypting files you've encrypted.

Alternatively, you might choose to install the same keys on two or more computers, so each is able to share encrypted files.

To do this, you need to export the key pair as a file.

If choose to do this, ensure you keep the key pair file safe because—perhaps obviously—anybody with the key file and your encrypted files will potentially be able to unlock them.

To export the key, first ensure the computer's time and date is correct (to learn how, see page 47). Then start the Password and Encryption Keys program. It can be found on the Applications ⇨ Accessories menu. Ensure the My Personal Keys tab is selected and right-click your key in the list. Click Properties in the menu that appears, and click the Details tab in the dialog box. Finally, click the EXPORT button at the bottom right, and choose a location to save the key file.

To import a key in a different Ubuntu installation, first ensure the time and date is correct on the computer. Then start the Password and Encryption Keys program, as described above, and click Key ⇨ Import on the menu. Finally, navigate to your saved key.

Enhancing web browser security

Ubuntu 8.04 and 8.10 use version 3 of the Firefox browser. This has significant security features, such as protection against phishing, wherein users are redirected to fake websites in order to steal login

Figure 7-2. Firefox reporting a phishing attack.

details, and protection against malware sites, where viruses or other dangerous files are offered surreptitiously. See Figure 7-2 for an example of what you'll see if you fall victim to a phishing attack (note that this is a staged demonstration at the `www.mozilla.com` site, and is not an actual attack; `www.mozilla.com` is safe to visit).

No configuration is necessary to utilize these features because they are enabled by default. However, in addition you might opt to activate the master password function, and install add-on software to block against script-based attacks, as discussed in the next sections.

TIP None of the features discussed below are unique to Ubuntu. The instructions provided will work equally well with Firefox installations on Windows or Mac OS X.

Enabling a master password

Like many browsers, Firefox 3 can remember login usernames and passwords for various sites, so you do not have to type them on each visit. However, anybody with access to your computer will therefore be able to access these sites using your details should you leave your computer unattended.

Setting a master password allows you to lock and unlock the password file in which usernames and passwords are stored. Whenever you start Firefox and visit a site requiring a password, you'll be invited to enter

---

the master password. Only when this is done will the website's username/password field be filled-in. When Firefox is quit, the password store is locked. It's only necessary to unlock the password file once each time you use Firefox.

TIP Because you're only prompted to unlock the password file once each time you use Firefox, it makes sense to get in the habit of quitting Firefox when you've finished with it, rather than leaving it open in the background.

To enable the master password, click Edit ➪ Preferences in the Firefox program window, click the Security heading at the top of the dialog box that appears, and put a check alongside Use a Master Password. Then type a new password, as prompted. When done, quit and restart Firefox. The changes will take effect immediately—when you visit a site requiring a username/password that Firefox knows, you'll be prompted for the master password.

Avoiding "executable content" attacks

Many websites make use of JavaScript, Java, and/or Flash to provide useful functionality. Such website features are known as *executable content*.

Unfortunately, in a minority of cases, executable content can be used to attack your computer and steal data. Because of this, many security-minded Ubuntu users opt to install NoScript, a Firefox add-on program that lets you authorize or restrict JavaScript, Java, Flash, and other technologies on a site-by-site basis.

Installing NoScript

To install NoScript, start Firefox and click Tools ➪ Add-ons. Ensure the Get Add-ons icon is selected in the dialog box that appears, and in the Search All Add-ons text field, type noscript. In the list of results, click the ADD TO FIREFOX button alongside the NoScript entry. In the dialog box that appears, click the INSTALL NOW button and, when installation has finished, click RESTART FIREFOX.

Blocking/allowing executable content

When Firefox restarts, you'll notice a new "S" icon at the bottom-right of the program window. Clicking this lets you enable or deny executable content for the site you're browsing. The default policy is for NoScript to deactivate everything, including Java, JavaScript, Adobe Flash, and Microsoft SilverLight components. However, some sites on a central whitelist are excluded from this protection, either completely or partially. These are sites considered trusted and reputable, and use executable content for vital site functionality. You can view and edit the whitelist by clicking Tools ⇨ Add-ons, clicking PREFERENCES alongside the NoScript entry in the list, and selecting the Whitelist tab when the NoScript dialog box appears.

Whenever you visit a new site that's not in the whitelist, and that contains executable content, a yellow bar will appear at the bottom of the browser window explaining what the objectionable content is. By clicking the OPTIONS button, you can choose to allow various elements. Provided you trust the website (i.e. it is reputable and you visit it often), you can usually select Allow All This Page [sic] from the menu. For example, I choose to allow all content on the www.bbc.co.uk sites, including BBC News (http://news.bbc.co.uk).

Alternatively, if you believe the site might have questionable or even malicious intentions, you can click Untrusted ⇨ Mark as Untrusted. This will mean the prompt about whether to allow content on the site will not appear should you visit the site in future.

Bear in mind that some sites look radically different without JavaScript or Flash. In particular, you may find some menu navigation systems fail to work correctly.

Glossary of terms

The following is a partial glossary of terms you're likely to encounter in this book, or in the Ubuntu community. The descriptions are contextualized for Ubuntu and no attempt is made to provide full definitions.

■ A

absolute path
A full description of the location of a file or folder, from the root of the filesystem upwards. See also *relative path*.

applet
In the context of the Ubuntu desktop, an applet is a small program with a narrowly-defined function (for example, displaying the time).

Apache
Web *server* software. See *LAMP*.

APT
Advanced Packaging Tool; the higher-level software management subsystem in Ubuntu. See also *dpkg*.

■ B

bash
Bourne-Again SHell; the default *command-line* *shell* used in Ubuntu and most versions of *Linux*. Based on the older *sh*.

binary

Source code that has undergone *compilation* into a program that can run natively on a computer. An *executable*.

BSD

Berkeley Software Distribution; a version of *Unix* originating at the University of Berkeley in the 1970s. Nowadays, it is available in several variations, including NetBSD, OpenBSD and FreeBSD.

■ C

C / C++

Programming languages used to create much of the *Linux* operating system *source code*.

client

A computer (or program) that connects to a *server*.

command-line

The line at which commands are typed in a terminal window or a *virtual console*. More often, the term refers to the overall interface and practice of entering commands, in contrast to using a GUI.

compilation

The process of turning *source code* into a *binary* file, normally using the *GNU Compiler Collection* (gcc) software.

config file

Short for *configuration file*; a file containing software settings.

cron

Service that allows tasks to occur at scheduled times, usually in the background.

CUPS

Common Unix Printing System; software that provides Ubuntu's printing functionality (including printer drivers). See www.cups.org.

■ D

Debian

Venerable community-generated *distribution* of *Linux* upon which Ubuntu is based, along with several other distributions of Linux. For more information, see www.debian.org.

dependency

Additional software needed for a program to work.

dependency hell

A situation where a user manually attempts to solve *dependency issues while installing or removing software, only to be presented with more dependency requirements.

desktop environment

Software that provides the graphical user interface, such as the desktop, trash facility, file manager, and so on. Examples available for *Linux include *Gnome, *KDE and *Xfce, but there are many others.

device file

Special files, usually contained in the /dev folder, that provide access to hardware, or a particular function provided by the kernel.

directory

Another word for a filesystem folder.

distribution

A version of the *Linux operating system. Shortened to "distro".

dpkg

Debian Packaging system; the basic software subsystem that gets software on and off the system. See also *APT.

dual-boot

If Windows and Ubuntu are installed on the same computer, it is said to dual-boot. A computer might also *triple-boot* if three operating systems are installed.

■ E

ext3

Underlying technology that provides the filesystem used within Ubuntu and many other *distributions of *Linux.

■ F

Free Software

Term devised by *Richard Stallman of the *GNU Project to identify software whose *source code is freely available for all to utilize, inspect, modify, and redistribute. See also *GPL.

fork

The splintering of a software project into two or more separate (often independent) projects. This is possible because of the nature of *open source* software, where the source code is freely available.

▓ G

Gnome

Desktop environment focusing on user-friendliness and non-technical users. See www.gnome.org. The term was once an acronym for *GNU Network Object Model Environment*, but this has been dropped. See also *KDE* and *Xfce*.

GNU

GNU's Not Unix; a so-called recursive acronym referring to the GNU operating system that attempts to recreate *Unix*. See *GNU Project*.

GNU/Linux

Another term for any operating system utilizing *GNU* software and with the *Linux* kernel at its heart. The term is preferred by *Richard Stallman* because it acknowledges the input of the *GNU Project*.

GNU Project

Seminal operating system project that recreates the venerable *Unix* operating system using entirely *Free Software*. See www.gnu.org.

GPL

GNU Public License; software license used by most *Free Software* projects that enshrines in a legal contract the right of users to view, study, modify, and redistribute the *source code* of software, along with future iterations. The *Lesser GPL* (*LGPL*) cedes some of the requirements of the GPL, and is usually used to enable the redistribution of library files.

grep

Global Regular Expression Print; *shell* command that offers powerful search features. In *Linux*/*Unix* circles, the word "grep" is synonymous with searching; to "grep a file" is to search through it.

▓ H

hack

A method of solving a problem, usually in an ingenious or makeshift way. See *hacker*.

hacker

A *programmer* or user of Unix (and by extension Linux). The term was hijacked by the media in the 1980s to refer specifically to computer criminals. Many true hackers object to this reclassification, and use the word *cracker* to describe such people.

■ K

KDE

K Desktop Environment; *desktop environment* utilized by *Kubuntu*, in preference to *Gnome*. See also *Gnome* and *Xfce*.

kernel panic

A crash involving the *Linux* kernel. Usually the words "kernel panic" appear on-screen when it occurs.

Kubuntu

Version of Ubuntu that uses *KDE* rather than *Gnome* for its *desktop environment*. A handful of graphical tools differ from the main Ubuntu release, but the projects are otherwise technically identical and are released to identical schedules.

■ L

LAMP

Linux, *Apache*, MySQL, and PHP; combination of software used on web *server* computers.

link

A method of providing a filesystem shortcut to a file. Links are either *symbolic*, or *hard*. The difference is technical but symbolic links are most widely used.

Linux

Technically speaking, Linux is the name of a kernel program. When used to describe an operating system, "Linux" describes a recreation of the *Unix* operating system, usually using *Free Software*.

log

A file containing details of various occurrences alongside the time/date they occurred. Used for diagnostic purposes.

▪ M

md5sum

Software that creates a unique checksum figure for a file by which it can be discerned if the file is complete and not corrupted or altered.

module

Software that can be inserted or removed from the *Linux* kernel to provide certain functions, usually although not always related to hardware. Similar to drivers under Windows.

mounting

The process of making accessible the filesystem of a storage device. For example, if you insert a USB stick, it will be mounted so that the user can access the files on it. All filesystems have to be mounted, including the root filesystem containing the *Linux* operating system. This is done very early in the computer's boot process.

▪ N

NFS

Network File System; software that allows the sharing of files across a network. Although still used in larger institutions, the *Samba* method of sharing files is more popular for smaller setups.

▪ O

open source

In the context of computer software, open source is similar to *Free Software* although the focus is often on simply allowing others to view and share *source code*; crucially, some open source licenses don't place a requirement to share modifications made to code.

▪ P

package

An archive file containing installable software, along with configuration information for the software.

partition

Portion of a disk, usually dedicated to a particular filesystem. Ordinarily, all operating systems exist within their own partitions.

process

How the system refers to currently running programs, or components of programs.

programmer

Individual (or organization) that creates software. Also known as a *developer*.

proprietary

In the context of *Free Software*, refers to software whose *source code* breaks one or more of the requirements of the *Free Software* definition.

PPA

Personal Package Archive; how some refer to a small software *repository* that contains the work of a particular developer.

R

regular expression

A way of precisely describing a search string using various symbols and/or protocols. Also known as a *regex*. Understanding regular expressions is a useful Linux skill.

relative path

A description of the location of a file or folder specified in relative terms to the folder currently being browsed. See also *absolute path*.

repository

Large collection of software *packages*, usually online. See *APT*.

root

In the context of the filesystem, the root is the bottom of the filesystem, indicated by a forward slash (/). The same as C:\ under Windows. The *root partition* is the hard disk *partition* that contains the Linux operating system files needed to boot.

root user

The administrator user account.

run level

The operational mode of *Linux*—what *services* are running, and therefore what functions are available to the user.

■ S

Samba

Background software that allows Ubuntu to access shared files/printers on Windows computers, and share files/printers itself.

script

Essentially, a chain of commands that form a basic program. Scripts are used extensively when *Linux* boots, in order to configure the system for the user.

server

A computer (or program) that shares data or resources with *clients*. Typical examples are web servers and file servers.

service

Any software that runs in the background to provide essential functionality for the user or operating system.

shell

Any software that allows a user to interact with a computer, although the term usually refers specifically to the *command-line*. See *bash*.

source code

Sometimes referred to as simply "the source"; the original listing created by a *programmer*. See also *compilation* and *binary*.

Shuttleworth, Mark

South African entrepreneur responsible for creating Ubuntu, as well as setting up the Ubuntu Foundation, which provides its official home. Additionally, he owns and runs Canonical Ltd, which commercially sponsors Ubuntu and several related projects. Canonical also provides paid support services.

ssh

Secure SHell; software that provides encrypted remote access to a computer.

Stallman, Richard

Almost legendary *hacker* who founded the *GNU Project*, along with the Free Software Foundation (FSF), an organization that furthers the cause of *Free Software*, a concept he also originated.

standard input, output, and error

In simple terms, standard input is the device that provides input at the *command-line*. Usually this equates to the keyboard. Standard output refers to the device that shows output at the command-line.

Usually this equates to the display. Standard error is like standard output, except it contains only error messages or warnings.

swap

Also known as virtual memory (or *paging file* under Windows); a file on the hard disk where the contents of memory can be temporarily cached to free-up physical memory for other software. Unlike Windows, the Ubuntu installer creates an entire *partition for swap use.

■ T

tar

Archiving software popular with *Linux/*Unix users. tar files aren't compressed by default, although the bzip or gzip software is often used to do so.

tarball

A tar file (informal).

TCP/IP

Transmission Control Protocol/Internet Protocol; networking technology used at the heart of *Linux, and the Internet.

terminal program

Program usually running in a *desktop environment that allows access to the *command-line. A *terminal emulator*.

Torvalds, Linus

Finnish national and *programmer (now resident in the US) who started the *Linux kernel project in 1991, and continues to both manage and contribute to it.

tty

Teletypewriter; how *Linux (and *Unix) refers to the *command-line prompt on a technical level.

■ U

Ubuntu

African personal philosophy emphasizing community and personal responsibility, popularized by Nelson Mandela in post-apartheid South Africa. It is from this philosophy that Ubuntu Linux is both inspired and takes its name.

Unix

Seminal operating system project created in 1969 by AT&T, initially as a research project, but then released as a commercial product. Successive iterations of Unix defined the ground rules for operating systems to the present day, and inspired clones such as *Linux and *GNU.

▦ V

vi

Text editor that runs at the *command-line. Nowadays a clone of vi called vim is commonly used, but this is still referred to as vi.

virtual console

Non-GUI method of accessing the Ubuntu *command-line, accessed by hitting Ctrl+Alt and F1-F6. A *virtual terminal*.

▦ W

Wine

Wine Is Not an Emulator; software that creates much of the Windows infrastructure, allowing some Windows programs to run on Linux.

▦ X

X

See *X.org*.

X.org

Organization that provides the X11 software that Ubuntu uses for its graphical subsystem. Often, X11 is referred to simply as *X*, or as the *X server*. This refers to the *client-server* model X utilizes.

Xfce

Desktop environment used by the Xubuntu version of Ubuntu. The goal of the Xfce project is to produce software that uses minimal computer resources but still provides features modern users expect. Xfce was once an acronym for XForms Common Environment, but this has been dropped. See also *Gnome and *KDE.

APPENDIX B

Learning more
and getting help

An important aspect of being an efficient Ubuntu user is knowing where
and how to get help and, generally speaking, help can be found in three
places: in print, online, and within Ubuntu itself.

Books and magazines

Linux is well-served by magazine publications. Amongst those
considered authoritative are *Linux Journal* (www.linuxjournal.com)
and *Linux Magazine* (www.linux-mag.com). Outside of the US, English-
language titles of note are *Linux Format* (www.linuxformat.co.uk),
Linux User & Developer (www.linuxuser.co.uk), and *Linux Pro
Magazine* (www.linux-magazine.com; known simply as *Linux
Magazine* outside the US).

Several PDF-based magazines are available too. *Full Circle Magazine*
covers Ubuntu exclusively and issues affecting the Ubuntu community.
It is community-generated and available free-of-charge. For more
information, see http://fullcirclemagazine.org.

Also worth reading is *Free Software Magazine*, published in a free PDF
edition roughly every two months and covering matters relating to the
world of Free Software, including but not limited to Linux. For more
information, visit www.freesoftwaremagazine.com.

In terms of books, for a complete guide to Ubuntu I recommend my
own book, *Beginning Ubuntu Linux* (www.apress.com/book/view/

1590599918). Now in its third edition, *Beginning Ubuntu Linux* was the first English-language book to cover Ubuntu. It went on to win a *Linux Journal* award for End-User/Non-Technical Book of the Year, and regularly tops the list of best-selling books of its publisher.

Also of interest might be my other book, *Ubuntu Kung Fu* (www. pragprog.com/titles/ktuk/ubuntu-kung-fu). Frequently topping the Linux best-seller list at Amazon.com, *Ubuntu Kung Fu* contains over 300 tips, tricks, hints, and hacks for Ubuntu users of all levels. It's a superb partner to *Ubuntu Pocket Guide and Reference*, and will help push your Ubuntu skills further while productively improving your Ubuntu experience.

Online help

Linux grew-up alongside the Internet, so it should come as no surprise that the best source of help for Linux newcomers is found online.

Forums

The hub around which the Ubuntu community gathers is undoubtedly http://ubuntuforums.org, a series of message-board forums dedicated to all aspects of Ubuntu use.

In addition to a fleet of expert moderators, many Ubuntu old-hands frequent the boards and are eager to share their wisdom and experience with those having problems. In addition, many create How To guides, relating particularly to the use of cutting-edge software, and these form an important part of Ubuntu's community documentation.

The key to getting the most from Ubuntuforums.org is to "do your research first". So says Matthew Helmke, one of the administrators of Ubuntuforums.org. "Search Google and the like," he continues, "Mention what you have found, as well as the results of any attempts you have already made to solve the problem."

Matthew also advises being clear in postings, and describing the problem completely—including in the subject line you choose. A subject title like, "Configuring wifi: WEP won't work" is more likely to garner a better quality of response than, "Help! It won't work!". Remain polite, even if somebody responds unpleasantly.

"Only ask one question at a time," continues Matthew. If you have more than one problem, create multiple postings, but don't post too much all at once. Nobody likes seeing five messages in a row from the same individual.

Above all, when the problem is solved, add a message to that effect. "If the solution was posted by someone in the thread," says Matthew, "Please thank them." You can thank a user by posting a message saying so, but you can also click the *Thanks!* icon at the bottom right of the helpful posting. This increases the user's "Thanks" count, and helps indicate trustworthy and valued community members.

If you should find the answer elsewhere, post a link, and explain how the information you found helped you. Contextualize it if necessary.

Above all, remember that Ubuntuforums.org acts as a massive store of wisdom relating to Ubuntu. Your posting boosts this effort.

Ubuntuforums.org isn't the only useful forum website, of course. I also recommended www.linuxquestions.org, a general Linux forums site with a strong Ubuntu section, but there are many others.

Mailing lists

In addition to websites, you might consider joining one of the many Ubuntu email lists. Once you've subscribed, any messages sent to the list are sent out to all members, which can number in the hundreds of thousands. Other members of the mailing list can then answer your question, either directly via email, or by creating another posting to the mailing list.

For a list of all the officially-supported mailing lists for Ubuntu, see https://lists.ubuntu.com.

Built-in documentation

As mentioned in Chapter 5, all versions of Linux include man pages. These are effectively technical documentation about how the software in question works.

Additionally, the creators of many programs sometimes create separate documentation that is often more informal, and this can be found in the /usr/share/doc folder.

Finally, many GUI programs have their own help files, just like with Windows. These can be accessed by clicking the Help menu.

Understanding man pages

Man pages are concise technical documentation, usually although not always written by the creator of the software in question, and designed to serve as a quick guide to using the software.

Most man pages describe command-line tools, but the authors of some GUI applications also create them.

> **TIP** The man pages for many basic commands, such as cd, can be viewed by typing man builtins.

Unfortunately for newbies, man pages take no prisoners. Not only are they written in technical and thorough language, but they also assume in-depth foreknowledge of how Linux works.

As mentioned in Chapter 5, the grep command searches for text in a file. However, a newcomer would have trouble discerning this from the description in grep's man page:

```
grep [OPTIONS] PATTERN [FILE...]
```

```
grep searches the named input FILEs (or standard
input if no files are named, or if a single hyphen-
minus (-) is given as file name) for lines containing
a match to the given PATTERN. By default, grep prints
the matching lines.
```

However, as complex as man pages might seem at first, they can be easily navigated provided a few simple rules are understood.

Terminology

You already know two terms that appear frequently in man pages—*argument* and *option*—because they were introduced in Chapter 5. To recap, an *argument* (sometimes referred to as an *arg* in man pages) is what you tell a command to work on (or with). This is usually a file or folder. A command *option* alters how a command works, and is usually a word or (more often) a letter, preceded by a hyphen (or two).

> **NOTE** Depending on what a command option does and its complexity, you may find an option has its *own set of arguments* that alter how that particular option works!

Three phrases occur frequently in man pages: *standard input*, *standard output*, and *standard error*. Known technically as *standard streams*, they have a specific and important meaning relating to how Linux operates.

Standard input is where a program takes input from, if a file isn't specified. Standard output is where the output of a program is sent. Standard error is similar to standard output but, as you might have guessed, contains only error output.

NOTE Standard input, output, and error are sometimes referred to as stdin, stdout, and stderr.

All you need to know is this: In simple terms, standard input usually equates to the keyboard, and standard output equates to the display.

With this in mind, let's re-examine the extract from grep's man page. It says that if no filename is supplied, grep will search standard input. In other words, if no filename is specified, grep will search what you type.

This ability to search what you type might seem of questionable usefulness. However, as mentioned in Chapter 5, it's possible to redirect or pipe input into a command. In actual fact, redirection and piping *replace standard input* (hence the terms *redirect* or *pipe*—input to a command is redirected, or piped in).

With this in mind, it's becomes clear we can redirect or pipe input into grep, or any command like it that can take standard input.

NOTE Additionally, we can redirect or pipe the *output* of a command provided it uses standard output, which is to say, it usually displays its results on screen.

The author of the grep command's man page knew all about standard streams, of course, and he wrote the description the way he did because he expected you to know it too. If he'd had to explain from scratch, it wouldn't have taken four lines to describe grep's function—it would have taken four pages.

Structure

man pages are split into headings, each one inset against the main text and bolded. Commonly-encountered headings are as follows, although a typical man page may include more or fewer than this selection:

Name: Name of the command and a brief summary of its function.

Synopsis: A hypothetical example of the command. Arguments and options are underlined and listed where they should appear. Anything in square brackets ([ ]) is optional. Pipes (|) separate choices where a variety of options can be specified. Ellipses indicate where more than one argument or option can be supplied.

Description: A concise and technical description of the command.

Options: Possible command options, and what they do.

Files: List of additional files the command uses, or requires (typically, configuration files).

Notes: Optional section that attempts to illuminate further the software or technology being discussed.

Bugs: Any limitations or bugs the user should watch out for; usually related to usage in highly untypical circumstances.

Example: Real-world examples of the command in use.

See Also: Other programs (and/or man pages) you might like to investigate that are related to the software in question.

READMEs and other documentation

Inside the /usr/share/doc folder, you'll find subfolders for practically every piece of software installed on the system. Inside each folder is documentation created by the person (or people) behind the software.

The files are usually plain text, although are sometimes compressed using gzip, in which case they'll have a .gz file extension. The less command can be used to view both compressed and ordinary text files.

Usually the list of files includes any or all of the following, and sometimes other files in addition:

README: These files provide informal notes about the software and its function. Sadly, they're not always present. Bear in mind that README files aren't written specifically for Ubuntu. Instead, they're written for any potential user of the software, whatever operating system they're using, which might not even be Linux.

changelog: A list of feature additions or other changes made in successive versions of the software.

TODO: Work yet to be done on the software.

AUTHORS: Who wrote the software, plus contact details.

copyright: Details of the copyright agreement for the software.

NEWS: Similar to changelog, although inclusive of general developments in the software, or the project as a whole.

Often there are separate versions of these files with a .Debian file extension. These are written by the *package maintainer*—the person who compiled the software for inclusion with Debian/Ubuntu. README.Debian files point out things to know if using the software with Debian/Ubuntu, or sometimes provide a concise stand-in for a non-existent official README file.

Index

Continue your Linux adventure by learning some *Ubuntu Kung Fu*!

... The best-seller that contains over 300 tips, tricks, hints, and hacks to improve productivity. Learn more as you work through the tips and become an expert user while vastly improving your Ubuntu experience. It's an ideal first step after *Ubuntu Pocket Guide and Reference*, and is even more readable and fun!

Available from **Amazon.com** and other good book stores!

www.pragprog.com/titles/ktuk/ubuntu-kung-fu
Published by The Pragmatic Programmers, Sept 2008
400 pages, ISBN: 978-1934356227

2790403

Made in the USA